MARKS OF THE BODY OF CHRIST

Marks of the Body of Christ

Edited by

Carl E. Braaten and Robert W. Jenson

WILLIAM B. EERDMANS PUBLISHING COMPANY

GRAND RAPIDS, MICHIGAN / CAMBRIDGE, U.K.

© 1999 Wm. B. Eerdmans Publishing Co.
255 Jefferson Ave. S.E., Grand Rapids, Michigan 49503 /
P.O. Box 163, Cambridge CB3 9PU U.K.

Printed in the United States of America

04 03 02 01 00 99   7 6 5 4 3 2 1

Library of Congress Cataloging-in-Publication Data

Marks of the body of Christ / edited by Carl E. Braaten and Robert W. Jenson
p.   cm.
Includes bibliographical references.
ISBN 0-8028-4617-3 (pbk.: alk. paper)
1. Church — Marks.   I. Braaten, Carl E., 1929-   .
II. Jenson, Robert W.
BV601.M37   1999

262'.72 — dc21   98-49966
CIP

Contents

Eucharist

Office of the Keys

Ordination

Catechesis

Discipleship

In Place of a Preface: Martin Luther on "Seven Marks of the Church"

The Children's Creed teaches us that a Christian holy people is to be and to remain on earth until the end of the world. This is an article of faith that cannot be terminated until that which it believes comes, as Christ promises, "I am with you always, to the close of the age" (Matt. 28:20). But how will or how can a poor confused person tell where such Christian holy people are to be found in this world?

First, the holy Christian people are recognized by their possession of the holy word of God. To be sure, not all have it in equal measure, as St. Paul says (1 Cor. 3:12-14). Some possess the word in its complete purity, others do not. Those who have the pure word are called those who "build on the foundation with gold, silver, and precious stones"; those who do not have it in its purity are the ones who "build on the foundation with wood, hay, and straw." . . . This is the principal item, and the holiest of holy possessions, by reason of which the Christian people are called holy; for God's word is holy and sanctifies everything it touches; it is indeed the very holiness of God. "It is the power of God for salvation to everyone who has faith" (Rom. 1:16), and: "Everything is consecrated by the word of God and prayer" (1 Tim. 4:5). . . .

We are speaking of the external word, preached orally by men like you and me, for this is what Christ left behind as an external sign, by which

Excerpts from "On the Councils and the Church," in *Luther's Works* (Concordia & Fortress, 1955-), vol. 41, pp. 148-68.

his church, or his Christian people in the world, should be recognized. We also speak of this external word as it is sincerely believed and openly professed before the world, as Christ says: "Everyone who acknowledges me before men, I will also acknowledge before my Father and his angels" (Matt. 10:32). There are many who know it in their hearts, but will not profess it openly. Many possess it, but do not believe in it or act by it, for the number of those who believe in and act by it is small — as the parable of the seed in Matthew 13 says that three sections of the field receive and contain this seed, but only the fourth section, the fine and good soil, bears fruit with patience.

Now, wherever you hear or see this word preached, believed, professed, and lived, do not doubt that the true *ecclesia sancta catholica,* "a Christian holy people" must be there, even though their number is very small. For God's word "shall not return empty" (Isaiah 55:11) but must have at least a fourth or a fraction of the field. And even if there were no other sign than this alone, it would still suffice to prove that a Christian, holy people must exist there, for God's word cannot be without God's people, and conversely, God's people cannot be without God's word. Otherwise, who would preach or hear it preached, if there were no people of God? And what could or would God's people believe, if there were no word of God?

Second, God's people or the Christian holy people are recognized by the holy sacrament of baptism, wherever it is taught, believed, and administered according to Christ's ordinance. That too is a public sign and a precious, holy possession by which God's people are sanctified. It is the holy bath of regeneration through the Holy Spirit (Titus 3:5), in which we bathe and with which we are washed of sin and death by the Holy Spirit, as in the innocent holy blood of the Lamb of God. Wherever you see this sign you may know that the church, or the holy Christian people, must surely be present, even if . . . you know nothing of its holiness and power — just as the little children know nothing of it, although when they are grown, they are, sad to say, estranged from their baptism, as St. Peter laments: "They entice with licentious passions of the flesh men who have barely escaped from those who live in error" (2 Peter 2:18). Indeed, you should not even pay attention to who baptizes, for baptism does not belong to the baptizer, nor is it given to him, but it belongs to the baptized. It was ordained of him by God, and given to him by God, just as the word of God is not the preacher's (except in so far as he too hears and believes it) but belongs to the disciple who hears and believes it; to him is it given.

Third, God's people, or Christian holy people, are recognized by the sacrament of the altar, wherever it is rightly administered, believed, and received, according to Christ's institution. This too is a public sign and a precious, holy possession left behind by Christ, by which his people are sanctified so that they also exercise themselves in faith and openly confess that they are Christian, just as they do with the word and with baptism. . . . Don't be led astray by the question of whether the man who administers the sacrament is holy. . . . The sacrament belongs to him who receives it, not to him who administers it, unless he also receives it. In that case he is one of those who receives it, and thus it is also given to him. Wherever you see this sacrament properly administered, there you may be assured of the presence of God's people. For as was said above of the word, wherever God's word is, there the church must be; likewise, wherever baptism and the sacrament are, God's people must be, and vice versa. No others have, give, practice, use, and confess these holy possessions save God's people alone, even though some false and unbelieving Christians are secretly among them. They, however, do not profane the people of God because they are not known; the church, or God's people, does not tolerate known sinners in its midst, but reproves them and also makes them holy. Or, if they refuse, it casts them out from the sanctuary by means of the ban and regards them as heathen (Matt. 18:17).

Fourth, God's people or holy Christians are recognized by the office of the keys exercised publicly. That is, as Christ decrees in Matthew 18:15-20, if a Christian sins, he should be removed; and if he does not mend his ways, he should be bound in his sin and cast out. If he does mend his ways, he should be absolved. That is the office of the keys. Now the use of the keys is twofold, public and private. There are some people with consciences so tender and despairing that even if they have not been publicly condemned, they cannot find comfort until they have been individually absolved by the pastor. On the other hand, there are also some who are so obdurate that they neither recant in their heart and want their sins forgiven individually by the pastor, nor desist from their sins. Therefore the keys must be used differently, publicly and privately. Now where you see sins forgiven or reproved in some persons, be it publicly or privately, you may know that God's people are there. If God's people are not there, the keys are not there either; and if the keys are not present for Christ, God's people are not present. Christ bequeathed them as a public sign and a holy possession, whereby the Holy Spirit again sanctifies the fallen sinners redeemed by Christ's death, and whereby the Christians confess that they are a holy people in this world under Christ. And those who refuse to be converted or sanctified again shall be cast out from this holy people, that is, bound and excluded by means of the keys, as happened to the unrepentant Antinomians.

Fifth, the church is recognized externally by the fact that it consecrates or calls ministers, or has offices that it is to administer. There must be bishops, pastors, or preachers, who publicly and privately give, administer, and use the aforementioned four things or holy possessions in behalf of and in the name of the church, or rather by reason of their institution by Christ, as St. Paul states: "He gave gifts to men" (Eph. 4:8). His gifts were that some should be apostles, some prophets, some evangelists, some teachers and governors, etc. The people as a whole cannot do these things, but must entrust or have them entrusted to one person. Otherwise, what would happen if everyone wanted to speak or administer, and no one wanted to give way to the other? It must be entrusted to one person, and he alone should be allowed to preach, to baptize, to absolve, and to administer the sacraments. The others should be content with this arrangement and agree to it. Wherever you see this done, be assured that God's people, the holy Christian people, are present. . . .

Just as was said earlier about the other four parts of the great, divine, holy possession by which the holy church is sanctified, that you need not care who or how those from whom you receive it are, so again you should not ask who or how he is who gives it to you or has the office. For all of it is given, not to him who has the office, but to him who is to receive it through this office, except that he can receive it together with you if he so desires. Let him be what he will. Because he is in office and is tolerated by the assembly, you put up with him too. His person will make God's word and sacraments neither worse nor better for you. What he says or does is not his, but Christ, your Lord, and the Holy Spirit say and do everything, in so far as he adheres to correct doctrine and practice. The church, of course, cannot and should not tolerate open vices; but you yourself be content and tolerant, since you, an individual, cannot be the whole assembly or the Christian holy people. . . .

Now wherever you find these offices or officers, you must be assured that the holy Christian people are there; for the church cannot be without these bishops, pastors, preachers, priests; and conversely, they cannot be without the church. Both must be together.

Sixth, the holy Christian people are externally recognized by prayer, public praise, and thanksgiving to God. Wherever you see and hear the

Lord's Prayer prayed and taught; or psalms or other spiritual songs sung, in accordance with the word of God and the true faith; also the creed, the Ten Commandments, and the catechism used in public, you may rest assured that a holy Christian people of God are present. For prayer, too, is one of the precious holy possessions whereby everything is sanctified, as St. Paul says (1 Tim. 4:5). The psalms too are nothing but prayers in which we praise, thank, and glorify God. The creed and the Ten Commandments are also God's word and belong to the holy possession, whereby the Holy Spirit sanctifies the holy people of Christ. However, we are now speaking of prayers and songs which are intelligible and from which we can learn and by means of which we can mend our ways.

Seventh, the holy Christian people are externally recognized by the holy possession of the sacred cross. They must endure every misfortune and persecution, all kinds of trials and evil from the devil, the world, and the flesh (as the Lord's Prayer indicates) by inward sadness, timidity, fear, outward poverty, contempt, illness, and weakness, in order to become like their head, Christ. And the only reason they must suffer is that they steadfastly adhere to Christ and God's word, enduring this for the sake of Christ: "Blessed are you when men persecute you on my account" (Matt. 5:11). They must be pious, quiet, obedient, and prepared to serve the government and everybody with life and goods, doing no one any harm. No people on earth have to endure such bitter hate. . . . They must be called heretics, knaves, and devils, the most pernicious people on earth, to the point where those who hang, drown, murder, torture, banish, and plague them to death are rendering God a service. No one has compassion on them; they are given myrrh and gall to drink when they thirst. And all this is done not because they are adulterers, murderers, thieves, or rogues, but because they want to have none but Christ, and no other God. Wherever you see or hear this, you may know that the holy Christian church is there, as Christ says: "Blessed are you when men revile you and utter all kinds of evil against you on my acccount. Rejoice and be glad, for your reward is great in heaven" (Matt. 5:11-12). This too is a holy possession whereby the Holy Spirit not only sanctifies his people, but also blesses them.

These are the true seven principal parts of the great holy possession whereby the Holy Spirit effects in us a daily sanctification and vivification in Christ, according to the first table of Moses. By this we obey it, albeit never as perfectly as Christ. But we constantly strive to attain the goal, under his redemption or remission of sin, until we too shall one day become perfectly holy and no longer stand in need of forgiveness. Everything is directed toward that goal. . . .

Now we know for certain what, where, and who the holy Christian church is, that is, the holy Christian people of God; and we are quite certain that it cannot fail us. Everything else may fail and surely does. . . . When the devil saw that God built such a holy church, he was not idle, and erected his chapel beside it, larger than God's temple. This is how he did it: he noticed that God utilized outward things, like baptism, word, sacrament, keys, etc., whereby he santified his church. And since the devil is always God's ape, trying to imitate all God's things and to improve on them, he also tried his luck with external things purported to make man holy — just as he tries rain-makers, sorcerers, exorcists of devils, etc.

PROCLAMATION

The Word That Kills and Makes Alive

GERHARD O. FORDE

I recall reading some time ago a prediction by a homiletician of note (James Stewart perhaps?) that if the Protestant Church ever dies the dagger that will be found in its back will be the sermon. Now it would be tempting to spend some time reflecting on the irony of that: The sword of the word turns against those who wield it? Was it perhaps a mercy killing? or even a suicide? Is the prospect more to be celebrated than mourned?, etc. But I shall not succumb to that temptation since my assignment assumes, I take it, at least the place if not immediately the vitality of proclamation as one of the signals revealing the presence among us of that community we call the body of Christ.

I do find it appropriate, however, to say something preliminary about the use of the concept of "marks" in this matter and context. I pay heed to Martin Luther in his insistence that the true church, the body of Christ, is hidden to sight for the time being, at the same time as it is revealed to faith now and will be manifest to sight in the end times. The body of Christ is a hidden/revealed reality. It is not particularly helpful in our context to use the categories of "visible" and "invisible" regardless of whether Luther or other reformers may occasionally have done so. "Visible and invisible" usually suggest a permanent dualism built into the very nature of things. "Spiritual" things, or "metaphysical realities," for instance, might be considered permanently "invisible" whereas material or physical things are visible. The hiddenness of the body of Christ is not like that. The dialectic of hidden and revealed has an eschatological cast. Indeed, the proclamation itself declares, promises, the eschatological reality. It is not in principle invisible; it is just not here yet. The proclamation is the harbin-

1

ger, the prophecy that can, for the moment, only be believed. The proclamation is, you might say, a "giveaway," in a double sense: It both discloses and gives to faith the reality it signifies. Indeed, it makes believers members of Christ and precisely as such is the "signal" of the body of Christ.

Luther insisted on the proclamation of justification by faith alone itself renders the church so justified *absconditus,* hidden. And it is not just hidden like a lost toy behind the sofa. It is hidden, on the one hand, because it intends so to be. In accordance with what the Roman Catholic Daniel Olivier has called Luther's "negative dialectics,"[1] it absconds, it hides itself from the eyes of this age precisely because it will not submit to the tyrannies of this age. And it is hidden, on the other hand, because it is too glorious, too wild for us to take yet. It is as when we hear the word of justification we get thrown out of kilter, unable really to know what to do with it or about it. Is it reallly free? Don't we have to do something after all? Etc., etc, and all those boring questions. We are left, as Luther often said, like a cow staring at a new gate, afraid to enter. It is there, perhaps we should say, but like those who watched the healing of the blind in the Gospels, we can't see. The body is hidden in this age — hidden, we might say, in the wounds of the crucified one. Faith's object is not a matter of sight. True sainthood is not recognizable in this age.[2] "What no eye has seen, nor ear heard, nor the heart of man conceived, what God has prepared for those who love him" (1 Cor. 2:9).

As with the hiddenness of God, this is no doubt as frustrating as it is fortunate. Frustrating since it eludes our grasp when we want to get a fix on it and bring it under our control. Fortunate because the hiddenness by the same token protects from the threat of ultimate ecclesiastical tyranny. It shatters restrictive boundaries and so prevents the kind of sectarian exclusivism based on visibility. As Luther put it in his reply to Murner,

> I therefore conclude that the Christian church is not bound to any one city, person, or time. And even though the unlearned mob — the pope with his cardinals, bishops, priests, and monks — does not want to understand this or let it be true, it is certainly true for me and for everyone

1. Daniel Olivier, "Luther's Challenge to Roman Catholicism," in Marilyn J. Harran (ed.), *Luther and Learning* (Selinsgrove: Susquehanna University Press, 1985), pp. 115-32.
2. See, for instance, Luther's rejection of Erasmus's argument that the works and miracles performed by those who advocated "free will" rendered their sainthood visible and thus substantiated their advocacy. *Luther's Works,* vol. 33, pp. 85-89.

2

else, even for the children in the street and all of Christendom in all the world.[3]

The proclamation of justification by works, however, has the opposite effect. It thinks to render the church visible. But then the church always threatens to become tyrannical. If you are saved by works, you must have something to show for it, some evidence of transformation, perhaps a building or two to put your name on, and so forth. Thus you are exposed to the scrutiny of the judge and the ecclesiastical tyrant and limited to the sort of visible boundaries that make sectarianism inevitable.

But, of course, this brings us to the question standing behind the matter of the marks. If the body is hidden how shall we know it? The answer comes in the doctrine of the marks or signs of the church. Though hidden, the body announces itself through its "external" marks. The Reformation tradition, following Luther, has made three marks primary: the preaching of the Word, Baptism, and the Last Supper. Sometimes Luther will add to the list, as in "On the Councils and the Church," and tally as many as seven, adding the office of the keys, the calling of ministers, public prayer and worship, and bearing the cross. In all of this the point is that what characterizes these marks is they are all acts of liberation in the ultimate sense of the word. I say "ultimate" here to indicate that the liberation in question is not to be confused with sundry political liberations, however beneficial they may be to society in this age and however much they may flow from ultimate liberation. The liberation in question is a liberation from sin, death, and the devil. If it is not that, it is no mark of the church. The true church, that is, reveals itself, shows its hand, breaks in upon us, in acts of freedom, not in acts of tyranny. Where the Spirit of the Lord is, there is liberty.

This brings us finally to our topic proper, proclamation as a mark of the body of Christ, the Christian Holy People, as Luther likes to say. That there should be such a body, a Christian Holy People, is not apparent to sight but an article of faith. This situation remains just that until the end of the age. "But," Luther asks, "how will or how can a poor confused person tell where such Christian holy people are to be found in this world? Indeed, they are supposed to be in this life and on earth, for they of course believe that a heavenly nature and an eternal life are to come, but as yet

3. *Luther's Works*, vol. 39, p. 219.

they do not possess them. Therefore they must still be in this life and remain in this life and in this world until the end of the world."[4]

The answer to the question comes in the assertion that holy Christian people are recognized by their possession of the holy word of God. Where the word of God is, there is the body, the holy people. For Luther this was the principal mark of the church. Even if, he can say, "there were no other sign than this alone, it would still suffice to prove that a Christian, holy people must exist there, for God's word cannot be without God's people and conversely, God's people cannot be without God's word."[5] However, possession of the word does not mean just having the Bible around or hanging onto it. Luther takes pains to stipulate more exactly what he means by a mark that is to make us aware of the pending invasion of the church into our business.

> But we are speaking of the external word, preached orally by persons like you and me, for this is what Christ left behind as an external sign, by which his church, or his Christian people in the world, should be recognized. . . . Wherever you hear or see this word preached, believed, professed, and lived, do not doubt that the true *ecclesia sancta catholica*, "a Christian holy people" must be there, even though their number is very small. For God's word "shall not return empty" Isaiah 55[11]. . . .[6]

To qualify as a mark of the church the word must be orally preached, and believed, professed, and lived.

But this word, it should be marked, is to be understood not as quiescent but as as the truly liberating word. Indeed, as we know from Luther's writings one should be prepared to encounter trouble when this word is preached. "This," Luther maintains, "is the thing that performs all miracles, effects, sustains, carries out, and does everything, exorcises all devils. . . ." Luther, as you can imagine, has a rich assortment of the devils it exorcises. These devils are for the most part precisely those lurking in the machinery of justification by works, grace-wrought or otherwise, the fruit of human attempts to make the church visible: "pilgrimage-devils, indulgence-devils, bull-devils, brotherhood-devils, priest-devils, mob-devils, insurrection-devils, heresy-devils, all pope-devils, also Antinomian-

---

4. Timothy F. Lull (ed.), *Martin Luther's Basic Theological Writings* (Minneapolis: Fortress Press, 1989), p. 545.

5. Lull, p. 547.

6. Lull, pp. 546, 547.

devils,"[7] all of whom depart only with furious raving and rampaging, as can be seen in the ranting of "Emser, Eck, Snot-nose (Cochlaeus), Schmid, Wetzel, Bumpkin, Boor, Churl, Brute, Sow, and Ass."[8] This orally preached — indeed offensive — word is the primary external mark of the body of Christ, the living, active word that exorcises the demons, liberates from tyranny, and generally upsets the normal course of affairs in a works-righteous world. Wherever there is this kind of trouble you can bet the church is around somewhere!

But now, of course, not just any kind of pious or moralistic prattle will do as a mark of the body. So the nature of the oral word must be stipulated even more closely. The oral preaching that Luther has in mind is, of course, the gospel, the word of promise and I think it fair to say, the eschatological word breaking into our present to do us in, to put an end to us as old beings both negatively and positively — to put a stop to what we are and what we have been up to and to give us an end, to make us new. And this brings me to what my assignment really directs me to, the matter of proclamation itself.

What is proclamation? What is so unique about it that it can be taken as a mark of the body of Christ and not just a mark of some other body, perhaps the body of the preacher or philosopher of religion who may be unloading on us? Without attempting to argue the case here — I think I have done that elsewhere — I shall simply say once again that when I attempt to put all the pieces together as I have learned them, out of historical study and theological reflection on matters exegetical and hermeneutical, I come up with the proposal that proclamation should be the attempt to *do the text to the hearers, to do once again in the living present what the text records as having been done of old.* Proclamation is doing once again what the biblical text authorizes and mandates us to do today. Proclamation is a very particular use of the words. What it calls on us to do is not merely to exegete the text, though that is certainly involved; not merely to explain what it means — venturing opinions about such explanations — though it will entail that; or by some trickery or other seek to make it relevant to old beings, though that must no doubt be given a nod; but finally to do once again what the text once did, thereby allowing the text itself to set the agenda for us.

Proclamation I take to be the announcement, the declaration in the

---

7. Lull, p. 547.
8. Lull, pp. 547-48.

living present, indeed the opening of the eschatological future or at least the foretaste thereof, that creates faith. A close secular analogy would be something like Lincoln's emancipation proclamation. It simply declared the new situation, and opened up a new future. Theologically and liturgically the absolution is the most explicit paradigm (a paradigm, not a legalistic straitjacket!) for proclamation. "I declare unto you the gracious forgiveness of all your sins in the name of the Father, the Son, and the Holy Spirit." One should note several things about this paradigm. Watch the pronouns. It is I to you, first to second person. It is not a prayer or a wish or a hope in general for "us," it is a declaration "for and thus to you." It is present tense. Although rooted in God's past action, it's not about the past; it takes place in the living present and has to do with the future. It is a word that does something. It is the present installment of the mighty acts of God.

Proclamation can therefore be understood as a doing of the text to the hearers. As such, proclamation is both more specific and broader in scope than preaching. The title "preaching" is usually limited to time in the pulpit and only *per analogiam* and often pejoratively extended to other sorts of pious (mostly moralistic) admonition. Not every sort of preaching is actually proclamation. Preaching can be didactic, apologetic, ethically exhortative, and so forth. Whereas proclamation is particularly focused in the preaching, it takes place abundantly elsewhere. The liturgy, of course, puts much proclamation on our lips and constrains us to do it even if we don't want to. The mutual consolation of brothers and sisters, the private exercise of the office of the keys, and so forth are prominent instances in which proclamation is to take place. The church leaves its mark when it proclaims.

But how are we to understand proclamation with reference to preaching? Proclamation in the sermon is a very particularized task. This is reflected historically in the insistence that preaching involves not just pious talk, however emotional, but rightly dividing the word of truth, employing the distinction between law and gospel so that a new kind of speaking comes to light: gospel speaking. The suggestion that proclamation be understood as doing the text to the hearers is an attempt to reinterpret and reapply the old law/gospel method so as to render it fruitful for a theory of proclamation for today. It is ultimately an attempt to work out a theory of proclamation that tries to use words eschatologically rather than ontologically as symbolic signifiers.

To do this I find it useful to go back behind the old law/gospel distinction to its original root in the distinction between letter and spirit and the hermeneutical ferment engendered thereby. We are all used, I expect, to hearing that the law/gospel method — usually caricatured as preaching so much law and then so much gospel and perhaps a bit of sanctification to rescue the whole in the end — doesn't work so well any more as a theory for preaching. But, of course, discarding it generally means that only law gets preached and the distinction is entirely lost. It should be realized, however, that behind the distinction is the persistent letter/spirit debate over the import of scriptural interpretation for the teaching and preaching of the church. As I have maintained on various occasions, the trouble with the law/gospel method is that cut loose from this ancient moorage it tends to be reduced to moralization and/or psychologization and degenerates into a technique for manipulating people — an attempt to frighten people into faith, literally to try to make Christians by scaring hell out of them!

Actually, however, the distinction between law and gospel in Luther's own development flows out of a redoing of the hermeneutics of letter and spirit. Historically speaking, the single most important passage for the interpretation and functioning of the scriptural Word in the church is that from 2 Corinthians 3:4-6, where St. Paul claims that our sufficiency is not from ourselves but from God who has qualified us to be ministers of a new covenant, not in the letter but in the Spirit, for the letter kills but the Spirit gives life. Prior to Luther, to make a long story short and, I fear oversimple, the idea that the letter kills but the Spirit gives life was usually taken in a Neoplatonic sense, the idea that the literal or historical "meaning" was not in and of itself sufficient. It was, as the saying goes, "dead letter." If one remained stuck on the level of the letter one would perish in this world where time finally runs out and everything eventually decays, dies, rots, and starts to smell. In the Neoplatonic scheme words were taken, rather, to be symbolic of transcendent, eternal meaning, the realm of "spirit." To escape perishing one had to get beyond dead letter to life-giving spirit. One had, you might say, to milk out the "spiritual lesson" or the "moral" of the story. And as you no doubt recall, this could be developed elaborately in terms of the fourfold senses or meaning of Scripture. Words, that is, were symbolic signifiers. They were used to point to what used to be (literal historical) and beyond that to symbolize, to give hints of the unknown realms above, whether metaphysical or in a "Christian" scheme, doctrinal.

Every hermeneutic, moreover, is a covert soteriology. To be saved one has to be rescued from the realm of the dead letter. That mostly means some sort of gnosis. There would be no proclamation in such a view, generally only teaching and that usually meant endless argument about interpretation which somebody would have to settle. In other words, the hermeneutic demands a magisterium, and is well on the way towards an ecclesiology to match.

In his struggles to fathom what the Holy Spirit was up to in Scripture Luther came to question this entire approach to the matter. He came to see that the 2 Corinthians 3 passage, to make a long story short again, was to be taken literally just as it stands. The passage had to do, as he rightly saw, with ministry, with proclamation. God has qualified us to be ministers of a new covenant, not according to the letter but according to the Spirit, for the letter kills but the Spirit gives life. The text talks about what the words do, not about what they might symbolize. They kill and make alive. That the letter kills was not due, therefore, to some metaphysical inadequacy in its symbolic task but rather to the very nature of the case. The history of God with his people culminates in the cross. That spells one thing for old beings: death. It is not dead letter, it is deadly. And only so can the Spirit make alive. So the focus shifts from what the words might mean *literaliter* to what they do. If you want to know what they mean you have to consult the literal, grammatical sense. It is a cliché to say that the Reformation returned to the literal sense of Scripture and rejected the fourfold method of exegesis. But as long as that is all one says, one has just paved the way for fundamentalism. The secret to the matter of proclamation lies in what the words do, not merely in what they mean. They kill and make alive. Rightly used they are to *do* the eschatological deed — putting an end to us, stopping the old and starting the new. They function to do the eschatological deed here among us in our present, not as symbolic signifiers of a transcendent realm of ultimately inaccessible meaning. Such doing, I would think, is the tell-tale sign of the body of Christ among us.

So the question about this mark of the body of Christ gets down to that of how we are to do the text to the hearers. This is not the place to lay out a full-blown theory of proclamation, but a few things must be said to make the point about the marks of the church.[9] How does one do the text? First of all, of course, one has to begin with some careful consideration and exegesis of the text. But one has to look for more than just the literal history. What I usually look for beyond what the text says or "means," is what it does. The texts, especially in the Gospels, are accounts of highly charged

---

9. For a fuller account of my approach to proclamation see *Theology Is for Proclamation* (Minneapolis: Fortress Press, 1990).

situations and will very often tell you what they did to the hearers and/or viewers. They were incensed; they were amazed, they glorified God; or they took up stones to kill (it is, after all, a dangerous business!). The task is to attempt in our own way to do what the text once did. That being the case, we ought as much as possible, I believe, to lead from the text and its agenda rather than some catchy story or emotional personal experience of some sort. There seems to be a modern dogma about preaching that one has to begin with some kind of story that makes the text relevant. Indeed, we have gotten to the point where the story has taken over the whole sermon, which is dignified by the title of "narrative preaching." The story becomes the text. The story sets the agenda and the text is usually reduced to the status of an illustration. Such procedure is a kind of slander against the text. The assumption seems to be that here we are stuck with this ancient bit of irrelevance and we have to sweat and strain to make it "relevant" to modern life.

But if we operate from the perception that the letter kills and the Spirit gives life, we ought to approach the matter differently. I tend wherever possible to look for the really nasty bit, the kind of thing that is likely to get one crucified, the hard saying, the offensive attack, the climactic pronouncement, the shocking miracle, the shattering of all expectations that sets everything on edge, and to lead from that. For that is the doing of the work of the law. It is not simply "laws" that cause trouble but the "letter," the *opera literalia dei,* the literal word as such that kills so that the Spirit can make alive. But then in the end that very killing word must be turned around to be preached as gospel. For the literal word is not a symbol of some transcendent truth. The Spirit is hidden in the letter, not in some metaphysical never-never land. The gospel is hidden in the hard saying. In that way it is the very eschatological gospel-word that cuts in on our lives and puts to death so as to give life.

Now, that is the theory. The final question, however, is, how does it work? Lecturing on preaching is something like lecturing on swimming. One reaches the point of diminishing returns awfully fast. To extend the prediction with which I started, we might say that if preaching ever dies, the dagger that will be found in its back will be the lecture on preaching! So, while I do have a lot more to say on the subject by way of theory, I shall spare you all that and try to nail down what I mean by taking a look at a couple of texts.

The first one I like to talk about is Matthew 13:44. The kingdom of heaven, we are told, is like treasure hidden in a field, which a man found and covered up; then in his joy he goes and sells all that he has and buys the field. I like to start with this text because it was out of a struggle with the text that the whole matter opened up for me. The temptation in striving to make a text relevant — to find some "meaning" in it — is always to turn it into something to do, to turn it, say, into a law text. Now it is pretty difficult to do that with this text — as it is, I think, in an ultimate sense, with virtually all the parables and sayings, and certainly with the miracles. But I suppose, if we try hard enough, we can manage to give it an aura of relevance. We might say, for instance: "If you plow your field faithfully, if you stick to it day after day, someday, somewhere you too will find your treasure! Life has its little surprises after all, and maybe some day you will get yours." You could wax eloquent and teary-eyed about sticking to it and waiting patiently for your chance.

Or, of course, one might latch onto the bit about selling all. *There* is something to sink your moral teeth into! You have really to get serious, surrender, don't give in to the lusts of the flesh, the materialism of modern society, etc., etc. The only trouble is that according to the text it was in his joy at having already found the treasure that he went and sold everything. His action sprang from his joy; it was not a condition for arriving at it. In general, as I was preparing to preach it seemed to me that I would only make a complete hash out of it if I tried to turn it into something to do. I would miss the point. I would lose the joy.

For what is the attack, the killing letter in a text like this? It is the disturbing and shockingly irresponsible fact that the man apparently doesn't do anything to deserve the treasure. He doesn't plan on it, he doesn't strive for it, he doesn't earn it, nothing. He just stumbles onto it one fine day in the utterly mundane affairs of his probably meaningless and most likely irrelevant life. You feel about him, perhaps, much like you feel about someone who wins a lottery or a sweepstakes: "Lucky stiff, what did he do to deserve that?" And, of course, the unspoken resentment is not far behind: "When do I get *my* chance? Will the prize crew ever knock at *my* door?"

Now if one is really to make this text function as it ought, one would have to use the words in proper fashion. Why, we ought to ask, should anyone get crucified for speaking such a parable? It would appear that to begin with one would have to preach to uphold the utterly shocking nature of the surprise. It can't be toned down or turned into something to do. One surely can't end the discourse by exhorting the hearers to go out and find some hidden treasure. That, surely, would be silly — maybe very pious-sounding, but silly. Even in the text we are told that the man covered the treasure up after finding it. It's hidden treasure and it stays that way — maybe an allusion to the very hiddenness attendant on speaking in parables, so that those whose ears have become fat shall not hear, and those who think they know shall not know. All avenues are closed, every door shut. There is nothing to do. It's about the mystery of the Kingdom. Here God is at work and no one else.

No doubt one has to use imagination a bit to grasp the offense here. Everyone in Jesus' day had, it seems, some formula or method for getting into or bringing in the Kingdom. There were Pharisees with their concern about law — now being foisted on us again, it seems, by our exegetes. There were Sadducees and their compromises. There were Zealots with their liberation theology. There were Essenes and their ascetically tuned apocalyptic hopes. And along comes Jesus and says that the Kingdom is like treasure hidden in a field, which a man out plowing just stumbles onto! Imagine the offense! All of that high-minded piety simply shoved aside!

Now when we get this far we are, of course, in trouble. The text has us cornered. Where in the world can we go from here? If the treasure belongs to God and is impenetrably hidden, what more can one say? What can one do about it all? Shall we just conclude piously with a prayer, perhaps, that something will come of it? In my struggles with the text it finally dawned on me. There is only one possible move left: I would have to have the guts (or the Geist!) to give them the treasure, to bring it into the present tense, to have the nerve to say, "You lucky stiffs! You have stumbled onto it! Jesus died for you and was buried, went into the blackness of death and was yet raised for you. There it is!" One has to make the audacious claim that this is the moment God has from all eternity been scheming about. Repent! Sell everything! There is a new day coming, a new creation, and you have just stumbled onto it. Imagine that!

Something like that is what I am trying to get at by doing the text. It is not explaining the text, although that is involved; not merely exegeting it, although I hope that is apparent; but finally turning it to proclamation, doing it so as to kill and make alive.

Having illustrated what I mean in the first text, I shall content myself with just a few observations on a second, the parable of the laborers in the vineyard. You all know the story. The laborers came at different hours but in the end they all got the same. And that, of course, is offensive enough! When I first preached on this text I recall using that word "They all got the same" as first the killing letter and then turned it over as the life-giving

Spirit. But the next time I used it I came to think that the real offense, the killing letter, comes when they go to the keeper of the vineyard and complain. This, they insist, is no way to run a vineyard. Apparently they had already formed something of a union! But the vineyard keeper just peremptorily replies: "Can I not do what I want with what is my own?" Bang! You're dead! In the first instance that is the killing letter. It cuts off and shuts up. But in the second instance I would as the proclaimer have to "turn it over" because it is the gospel. I would have to proclaim the fact that indeed "the keeper of the vineyard" is going to do what he wants with you and that we can thank God for that because that's the only real chance we have. So I would have to have the audacity to claim that I am here to tell you just what it is that he has decided to do about you. "You are his own and he will never let you go." So were I to preach on that text I would most likely start right out with the hard saying: "Can I not do what I want with what is my own?" and drive home the offense, the killing function of that saying, and then turn it over. The Spirit is hidden in the letter, as Luther claimed. Proclamation is doing the text, doing the eschatological word to the hearers.

To conclude, my point in saying this, if I have not already made myself clear, is that today, at least, it is not enough just to go on and on in some sort of pious prattle and pretend that this is a mark of the body of Christ. The true mark is the eschatological word that kills and makes alive, that puts an end to the old and calls the new to life. The body of Christ will be remarked in the world only when such a word is heard.

Resurrection and Rhetoric

RICHARD LISCHER

Every Sunday, like clockwork, the room gets quiet. The ritual begins. Mothers or fathers of small children pull out the Ziploc bags with shards of toast and raisins and begin rationing them to preschoolers. Older members of the congregation fine-tune their hearing aids. Teenagers share one last secret with one another before turning to give the preacher their undivided attention for thirty seconds. The word is near you. It is about to be uttered.

A few days earlier the preacher enacted a similar ritual. She did exegetical and theological investigations of a passage of Scripture. She listened to the voices of her parish and to her own heart. She watched CNN for the latest-breaking news and scandals. The preacher finally closed the commentaries, turned off the TV, and said, "Now what? What word shall I utter?"

The preacher may find himself walking around an empty room or standing in a deserted sanctuary. He is full of faith but empty of the kind of power that is supposed to attend God's word. "The word is near you, on your lips and in your heart (that is, the word of faith which we preach)" (Rom. 10:8). So near that you can feel the breath of its power on the back of your neck, but also so elusive that you can think of absolutely nothing to say.

Little is said in the New Testament about the difficulty of preaching. We never meet a preacher who is having trouble thinking of something to say. Preaching may be a dangerous activity in the New Testament, but never difficult. That it will be accompanied by suffering is taken for granted. Paul simply portrays the word of God as an act of power and identifies that power with the death and resurrection of Jesus as it is mediated to the church by the Holy Spirit. When words get hitched to that event, something happens, something whose depth and richness cause other forms of discourse to pale by comparison.

This is the New Testament's theology of preaching. It offers no explanation of or rules for preaching but only the affirmation of a mystery in which we are privileged to participate.

This sounds rather abstract until we realize that it is precisely the power that we seek in preaching. In fact, when we place our preaching against an ideal norm, we are most frustrated by the powerlessness of our speech to effect real change. We want to participate in this mystery. I don't want to get up Sunday after Sunday, just me, armed with little more than my own limited range of ideas and my own personal foibles. I want my message to be a part of something larger than my talent.

The discipline of homiletics also recognizes the urgency of this desire, but ironically, it often turns to rhetoric for its satisfaction. I have been teaching homiletics for eighteen years, and it has been fun to watch the design schemes come and go with the regularity of Paris fashions or Yankee managers. We have fiddled with points, stories, moves, and style in search of the perfect glass slipper of *form*, hoping against hope that it will transform the dullest sermon into an exciting princess. However, I am reminded of the line from Robert Frost: "I gave up fire for form/till I was cold."

Let us join the theology of preaching with the language of preaching, as signified by the words *resurrection* and *rhetoric*, because these represent the two poles of Christian preaching. At first they don't seem to have much in common. Resurrection is a powerful eschatological event by which God raised Jesus from the dead. (Because of the nature of the death from which he was raised, namely, death on a cross, whenever we use the word *resurrection*, we mean cross and resurrection.) Resurrection is also a future event in which Christians hope. When we confess, "I believe in the resurrection and the life," we are Janus-faced, looking backward and forward at the same time.

When we use the word *rhetoric* we are talking about a strategy of language. Rhetoric is the words, designs, gestures, images, stories, arguments — everything we say to convey the life that was created by the resurrection. For example, when you hear the preacher deftly comparing the experience of waiting at the end of the line outside a movie theater to the parable of the workers in the vineyard, you know that she does not do so in order to share a childhood memory but to make the kingdom more real for her listeners.[1] There are, then, these two sides of preaching: one is the explosive but unpicturable event of the resurrection of Jesus, and the other is the words we craft in the sermon.

Let me use an analogy: rhetoric is the light that illuminates a beautiful room with a flick of the switch. If you did not understand the nature of electricity you might think that the switch contains all the magical powers necessary for light. The resurrection is the vast waterfall hidden deep in the mountains whose sheer power gives light to the entire valley. I offer this analogy to those who have experienced both sides of the church's preaching, who know both the ineffable power *and* the struggle for the words.

I have three reasons for stressing the theology of preaching (by which I mean understanding how God's revelation makes preaching possible, necessary, and effective). The first is that when preaching is spoken of exclusively in terms of technique, one is tempted to reduce preaching to communication, as if communication — and not the truth — were an end in itself. As we know, there is no lack of communication in the Information Age. But truth is as scarce as it ever was.

The second, related, reason for focusing on the theology of preaching is found in the Bible's own God-centered approach to preaching. We speak because we have a speaking God, *deus loquens.* If there were stage-directions attached to the Old Testament they would read, *Enter God, talking.* Jeremiah issues the ultimate put-down of the gods of neighboring tribes. He says, "Their idols are like scarecrows in a cucumber field, and they cannot speak" (Jer. 10:5a).

This theology comes with no operating instructions. In the New Testament we have no complete sermons (as we know them). We have two-minute outlines of sermons in the Book of Acts — for example, Paul's address at Pisidian Antioch in which he retells the history of salvation climaxing in the resurrection, quotes Psalm 2, and issues several appeals and warnings (13:16-41). On other occasions, the apostle goes out of his way to warn the Corinthians *not* to evaluate his sermons on their rhetorical merits: "I did not come proclaiming to you the testimony of God in lofty words or wisdom. I decided to know nothing among you except Jesus and him crucified" (1 Cor. 2:1-2). For which he received some bad sermon evaluations: "For they say his letters are weighty and strong, but his bodily

1. Barbara Brown Taylor, "Beginning at the End" in Thomas Long and Cornelius Plantinga, Jr. (eds.), *A Chorus of Witnesses* (Grand Rapids: Eerdmans, 1994), p. 15.

presence is weak and his speech is of no account" (2 Cor. 10:9). All that we can conclude about preaching from the apostle's comments is that he told the story simply, from the Scriptures, that he trembled at the implications of his own message, and that the crucifixion and resurrection of Jesus were the heartbeat of his homiletics.

My third reason for being concerned with a theology of preaching is pastoral. How to put it delicately? People are dying. People are dying, and they can't be exhorted back to life again. They cannot be nagged back to life. They can't be entertained or massaged back to life again. They have to be raised from the dead. One of my favorite stories in the New Testament is in Mark 4. It takes place in a boat in which Jesus is asleep in the stern. A storm is raging. When the disciples awaken him, they speak (in the King James Version) like an English butler: "Master, carest thou not that we perish?" The Greek can be translated, however, "We are dying," with the force, as one commentator notes, of "inevitable doom." "We are going down and only you can save us." We are dying of hate as well as cancer. We are dying of despair as well as disease. But make no mistake about the "dying" part. Preaching owes those who are dying a word of life.

From the very beginning the resurrection was a speaking event. At no time does the resurrection of Jesus lie fallow as an unproclaimed fact about which one might muse, "Isn't that interesting?" The resurrection is the result of a metaphorical call: God called forth Jesus from the tomb, an event foreshadowed by another cry, "Lazarus come out!" all of which was made possible by a creative call to the primordial chaos, "Let there be. . . ." The disciples do not decide to preach because they have come to their senses but because they have been preached to first by the angel, then by the risen One. We exist as a church because we have been "called out." Bound up with the event — more words — is the commission to "go and tell," to baptize, and to make disciples. The angel seems to be saying, "Look, there is a kind of speech that is commensurate with this new event called *risen*. It is risen speech. Your speech did not create this event, but it completes it." Theologian Carl Michalson was surely right when he said, "[T]o be a Christian is to be involved in the problem of the communication of the gospel."[2]

Linguistic philosophers tell us that any kind of creative speaking is like a resurrection in that it creates some new insight, relationship, or atti-

---

2. Carl Michalson, "On the Gospel" in Richard Lischer (ed.), *Theories of Preaching* (Durham, N.C.: Labyrinth [Baker Books], 1987), p. 33.

tude. There is a sense in which nothing exists for us until it is spoken. For example, the prophet speaks to a rigidly segregated nation that has no image for what he is about to say: "I see a day," he cries, "when black people and white people will sit down at table together and treat one another as kin because they *are* kin." From that moment, the reality of brotherhood and sisterhood begins to exist, because someone has articulated it.[3] It is impossible to do something that has never been said. Such is the power of risen speech.

You attend a wedding, and if you don't hear the words "I now pronounce you husband and wife," you're not positive anything has changed. Even people who know that they are forgiven by God find it necessary to say, "In Jesus Christ, you are forgiven."

About three days after I was ordained, I was called in the middle of the night to a hospital I didn't know in a town fifteen miles away, where a woman I didn't know had a rupturing gall bladder. I got lost on the back roads and in the fog, and when I arrived at the hospital at so late an hour I had a difficult time gaining entry. When I rushed to her room, she and her husband were gone. I dashed through several NO ADMITTANCE doors to the OR, which was closed. I found her gurney parked in a small dark laundry alcove nearby. It was a dingy little space with nothing on the wall but a religious picture of St. Joseph and a fire extinguisher. My parishioner was disheveled and scared. Her husband said, "Thank God you are here," as if I had just landed in a jet to perform the surgery. She had large, frightened eyes, and I, three days into the ordained ministry, did not know what to say. All that came to me was the liturgy. So I said, "The Lord be with you." They replied, "And with thy spirit." I said, "Lift up your hearts," and they said, "We lift them to the Lord." Suddenly what was disheveled and panicked regained its order, and the Lord was once again the Lord of the alcove. The presence of God among us was palpable. I don't think I "preached" in the alcove, but the word created something that sustained two frightened parishioners and one inexperienced pastor. Such is the power of risen speech.

Every Sunday the word of preaching breaks into the silence of a room gone still. Metaphorically speaking, those who proclaim the risen Christ give voice to those who are dead and to those who are alive but languish in silence. "Prophesy to the bones," the Lord says to Ezekiel, "and say,

---

3. Richard Lischer, *The Preacher King: Martin Luther King, Jr. and the Word that Moved America* (New York: Oxford, 1995), p. 10.

'O dry bones, hear the word of the Lord.'" It is no accident that so many of the great expressions of the gospel are spoken in cemeteries. Whenever I visit my friend in the nursing home, I am always shaken by how quiet it is there. The place needs music, children, and laughter. Jeremiah's final portrait of doom is the picture of a silent world.

Preachers get as nervous as any with prolonged silence. We have filled the silence with bold affirmations of our personal survival. The gospel certainly has to do with our persons and with our survival. But resurrection is a bigger event than that. It first witnesses to God's own divinity. To raise anything from death is exactly what one might expect from the God who mastered the chaos, created Leviathan, or parted the waters of the Red Sea. The raising of "this Jesus," as Luke puts it in Acts 2:32, testifies to God's faithfulness to those whom he has chosen.

Resurrection also witnesses to God's commitment to the whole creation, especially those who suffer sickness, poverty, and oppression. Theologian Miroslav Volf has written an article with the unlikely title, "The Trinity Is Our Social Program." He wants to indicate that the interpenetrating love of the three persons of the Holy Trinity is not a piece of abstract theology separated from our social and political commitments, but it potentially orders all our duties and relationships.[4] Thirty years ago Volf's teacher Jürgen Moltmann made a similar argument for the resurrection of Jesus. In too many theologies the resurrection is literally an appendix to the life and teachings of Jesus. No one knows what to do with it. Moltmann argued that because God was fully incarnated into this world, his crucifixion takes up the suffering of all, and his resurrection effects God's own protest against suffering.[5] If you want to know where God stands on AIDS, Rwanda, crack-cocaine, land mines, and death itself, look at the open tomb. The resurrection is our social program.

Now, WHAT KIND of preaching does the resurrection produce? What is the connection between the theology of preaching and the Sunday sermon?

When famed explorer Jacques Cousteau died, one of his associates said, "He had a very different view of the world. For him the real world existed beneath the surface. His genius was that he enabled us to see this

---

4. See Miroslav Volf, "The Trinity Is Our Social Program," *Modern Theology* 14, 3 (July 1998).

5. See Jürgen Moltmann, *Theology of Hope*, trans. James W. Leitch (New York: Harper & Row, 1967).

other world." If you listen to the media voices in our culture, you can't help but appreciate how very deep and different is the language of preaching. The spin doctors keep to the surface; the preacher is required to plumb the depths in order to impart a different view of the world.

Preaching presents an alternative to the unresurrected chatter of our culture. One of the vexing things about our sensorium is that every claim we make for words our culture affirms and absorbs. When we decry the suffering of the world, politics replies, "We feel your pain." If we say, "Language creates a world," Madison Avenue says, "Indeed it does." If we preachers say, "Images are so important," CNN replies, "We think so too." "Yes," we counter, "but our word is one of death and resurrection," and before the words are out of our mouth we meet them in greeting cards and aphorisms Scotch-taped to locker-room walls.

We are getting absorbed into someone else's world. It is the world of easy information, the dominant symbol of which is the monitor, the screen, by whose flickering light every knowledge is available and any experience is possible. It is the world of psychological explanation, by whose wisdom all is understood and all is forgiven. It is the world of democratic capitalism, which guarantees a common set of values and a universal language to express them. It is the world of spirituality that rounds off the rough edges of ancient creeds and exclusive claims. The only hedge against total absorption is the priority of the Christian proclamation. If we don't start *from* Christ we will never get *to* Christ.

In recent decades homiletics has been uniformly critical of sermons that begin with the priority of the word of God, preferring instead to build the sermon on the authority of the needs, capacities, and experiences of the listener. A good example is the book *Naming Grace* by Mary Catherine Hilkert, in which we are advised to look for "signals of transcendence" and to name the grace that is sacramentally present in all human experience.[6] This advice recaps the theme of mainline homiletics for the past thirty years. What the Catholic Hilkert renders in more acceptable sacramental terms, Protestant liberals have been saying for years. And now even evangelicals are asking how the sermon can service the anxieties of aging Baby Boomers or the indifference of Generation Xers. The common solution appears to be: Scratch deeply enough into the postmodern psyche and you will hit a vein of genuine spirituality. One way to tap into it is to tell stories whose religious

---

6. Mary Catherine Hilkert, *Naming Grace: Preaching and the Sacramental Imagination* (New York: Continuum, 1997), pp. 49-50.

dimension is recognizable and acceptable to all, and then to correlate the experience generated by these stories with the Christian message, e.g., "grace." When done successfully, the presence of Christ radiates as a spiritual dimension of everyday life. When the reliance on experience dominates the sermon, the gospel becomes an illustration of a greater truth.

A recent book by the sociologist Marsha Witten substantiates this disturbing trend in Christian preaching. In her book, *All Is Forgiven: The Secular Message in American Protestantism,* Witten analyzes forty-seven Presbyterian and Southern Baptist sermons on the parable of the Prodigal Son for their secular assumptions. Her conclusions are depressingly predictable. She finds that the preachers have accommodated the Bible's own words about God, sin, forgiveness, and reconciliation to the privatization of faith, therapeutic concerns, and utilitarian religion.[7]

For example, she notices that more than one preacher turns the Prodigal Son into a victim of the complexity of the modern world or tells the story as a classic example of sibling rivalry. One concludes that it's a healthy move for him to get out from under his older brother's shadow.

She notes that many of the preachers proclaim the psychological or social benefits of being a Christian without regard for the faith's integral elements such as cross, resurrection, discipleship, and obedience. It is interesting to note that in the first chapter of her book Witten personally dissociates herself from the Christian faith whose language she is about to analyze. By the last chapter, however, it is the nonbelieving social scientist who concludes her study with an expression of concern for the integrity of Christian preaching.[8]

Perhaps the greatest effect of the resurrection on preaching is found in the preacher rather than the sermon. It is a glorious effect. The preacher is set free from the burden of preaching. In his lectures on homiletics, Karl Barth says that the preacher stands between two advents, the first and second coming of our Lord.[9] He means that the preacher is not condemned forever to making relevant a figure from the ancient past. Can you imagine any greater burden than having to conjure a meaningful Christ from old materials? To make him *real?* No wonder preachers burn out, if they think they have to produce a relevant God for a demanding audience. Standing

7. Marsha Witten, *All Is Forgiven: The Secular Message in American Protestantism* (Princeton: Princeton University Press, 1993), p. 60.

8. Witten, p. 140.

9. Karl Barth, *Homiletics,* trans. Geoffrey Bromiley and Donald E. Daniels (Louisville: Westminster/John Knox, 1991), p. 54.

between two advents means that the subject matter of our speech is not always receding into the murky past (as all things historical must) but is waiting to meet up with our words.

We could not have preaching at a funeral if we did not recognize the risen Christ out ahead of our grief. We could not speak a courageous word about justice based only on the Hebrew prophets or our own indignation, if we had not already met Christ out ahead in the poor, the homeless, and the incarcerated. Preaching is a way of joining up with the new creation already in progress. The discipline of homiletics should not only teach the rules of sermon-writing but help form persons who will know Jesus when they meet him in their ministries.

If we speak under the sign of death and resurrection, something in our preaching will die as well. What dies is the centrality of the preacher's ego in the event of preaching. What dies is the scavenger hunt for originality, the antithesis of which was the ancient church's practice of reading the sermons of others. What dies is the quest for *my personal style,* which is contradicted by Augustine's revolution in homiletics by which he insisted that preachers allow their style to be determined by the *style* of the text.[10]

Resurrection preaching belongs to something larger than my personal ability to generate joy in an audience. Think of preaching as a conversation at an enormous, glittering, delightful party. You and I arrive many centuries after the party has gotten under way and will, alas, depart long before it is over, but while we are there how blessed we are to take a small part in the conversation.[11]

One Sunday morning last summer we had a service at Duke Chapel with the title, "Cancer Survivors' Sunday." Officials of the university's hospital persuaded the Chapel that such a gesture would improve town-gown relations, and, since nothing much happens in the dead of summer anyway — why not? The service turned out to be another Easter Sunday, with people crowded onto the back steps and standing in the aisles. I found a place to sit in a concrete niche at the back of the west transept, beside a young man from Korea. The sermon, which addressed the story of the storm on the Sea of Galilee, caused us all to think of God's presence in the midst of suffering. As we prepared for the eucharist we exchanged the peace of the Lord. A few minutes later, the young man next to me leaned over and with

---

10. *On Christian Doctrine,* IV, pp. 6ff.

11. Kenneth Burke's characterization of rhetoric in *The Philosophy of Literary Form,* 3rd ed. (Berkeley: University of California Press, 1973), pp. 110-11.

no introduction said, "I had a friend who committed suicide. What do you say to that? I wonder what I could tell 'my friends' to answer that?" We had a long and thoughtful conversation in which we bore witness to one another. In fact, if others noticed, they might have thought us ill-mannered, for this conversation continued in animated fashion as we stood in line and approached the table, only ceasing long enough for us to receive the body and blood of the risen Lord. In that case, the verbal proclamation was making antiphons all over the church. And the church, through its identification with the cancer sufferers, its eucharist, its mutual care and fellowship, and all the other "marks" of its existence, was manifesting the resurrection. The best resurrection preaching, then, occurs when the whole church is the preacher.

When Jesus came out of the tomb, the church came out with him, and it came out talking, singing, praying, and suffering. To say that the sermon should fit its environment is to say something that any classical orator would have accepted. But when we say that risen speech dies to itself, we mean that it does not find its completion in personal approval or even conversion, but only in ecclesial action. The sermon spends itself in *diakonia* in the world.

If something must die in such preaching, something else must rise. Here one is tempted to say that every sermon should express the joy of victory, that the preacher should be unfailingly upbeat, and let it go at that. Powerful, positive, purposeful preaching! Let every sermon be an "Ode to Joy" with no minor chords allowed. But, as Rowan Williams so astutely points out, the resurrection doesn't just cancel the crucifixion, with glory replacing defeat, but real joy arises *from* despair.[12]

In a sermon on the burial of Jesus, Paul Tillich tells the story of a man who testified at the Nuremberg Trials of how he had fled a camp near Wilna, Poland, and had been forced to live in a Jewish cemetery. In one of his poems he described a young woman in a nearby grave giving birth to a baby. In her delivery she was assisted by an old man dressed in a shroud. When the newborn uttered its first cry, the old man lifted the child to heaven and said, "Great God, hast thou sent the Messiah to us? For who else than the Messiah himself can be born in a grave?"[13] Who indeed?

12. Rowan Williams, *Resurrection* (London: Darton, Longman & Todd, 1982), p. 101.
13. Paul Tillich, "Born in the Grave" in *The Shaking of the Foundations* (New York: Scribners, 1948), p. 165.

THOSE WHO PREACH the resurrection do so from territory that has not been fully liberated. Resurrection preaching features joy with an edge, an in-your-face, "nevertheless" quality — like a friend I had who went dancing the night before she was to begin her third round of chemotherapy. The best dancing is done on the devil's dance floor.

Williams also notices that the episodes surrounding the resurrection of Jesus contain language that is both familiar and "odd."[14] Jesus is perceived an ordinary gardener, but he is also a stranger who can't be held. The risen Christ passes through doors, and yet he bears three-dimensional wounds in his flesh. He walks on water like a phantasm, and he cooks real fish over an open fire. But strangest of all, we can only proclaim his presence in his physical absence.

Is it possible for our sermons to be as real and as *odd* as the New Testament? We continue its strangeness by proclaiming the peace of Christ to people in the midst of social, race, gender, and culture wars. We announce the victory of Christ in dingy hospital chapels and cemeteries. We celebrate an organic relationship with one another in a society of individuals. We practice obedience in a culture dedicated to rights. We claim that an event that happened to one person long ago is somehow available to us in a form other than history.

Many of us were trained to remove any trace of oddness from the Christian message. We learned to make sermon illustrations that associate Christian truth with universally recognized truths, whether in psychology, politics, or morality. We clutter our sermons with "illustrations" of famous heroes, but the examples of ordinary saints are left on the cutting room floor. Somehow, *they* are not real. We tacitly accept the world's definition of "the world"[15] and humbly try to accommodate the gospel to it, as if the cross and resurrection have not deranged the old world and started a new one. We preach *in* churches, but too rarely do we depict the world *of* the church with a reality, language, and goodness of its own. Those who listen to sermons long to see a believable world of Christians depicted in them, one in which they have a speaking part.

Popular spirituality prefers nuggets of inspiration to eschatology or serious talk about discipleship and suffering. The preacher can't help but

14. Williams, p. 73.

15. See Stanley Hauerwas, "The Church in a Divided World: The Interpretive Power of the Christian Story" in *A Community of Character* (Notre Dame: University of Notre Dame Press, 1981), pp. 91-92.

envy other users of words in our culture. Politicians, gurus, lawyers, comics, pundits, savants: They are *so* smooth. They have but to open their lips and out flows — the spirit of the age. Preachers, on the other hand, often appear to be out of place or distraught, as though fighting off a swarm of bees. Their language emerges from pastoral participation in the struggles between life and death. Commenting on the syntactically broken style of speech in the Apostle Paul, Joseph Sittler observes, "Where grammar cracks, grace erupts," and then he adds a word of warning, "What God has riven asunder let no preacher too suavely join together."[16]

It is not the business of theology to dictate style. But the resurrection of Jesus does have a rhetoric, and we are only beginning to see its contours. We are only beginning to notice how strange it is when compared to our own homiletical instincts. And we are not a little astonished at what risen speech can mean to those who live in a dying world.

16. Joseph Sittler, "The Role of the Imagination" in Lischer, *Theories of Preaching*, p. 247.

BAPTISM

Baptism as a Mark of the Church

SUSAN K. WOOD

The subject of this conference is uncannily as subversive as it is accurate. The title of the conference is "Marks of the Church," and yet this presentation is on baptism. Within the tradition, the marks of the church are those listed in the Creed: "one, holy, catholic, and apostolic." Nowhere does the Creed name sacraments as marks of the church. In the Roman Catholic tradition, at least, we are not accustomed to thinking of sacraments as marks of the church. Martin Luther, however, listed seven practices constitutive of the church, including baptism, and called them "marks of the church."[1] This occasion invites me to consider whether sacraments belong to the individual or to the church, whether they are marks of an individual or marks of the church. They are both, of course, but within a privatized theology of the sacraments, the answer tends to come down on the side of the individual, and their identity as marks of the church are forgotten. However, I argue that in terms of a unified rite of initiation, the answer comes down on the side of the church, and I will explore baptism from this point of view. In doing this I will argue that the ecclesial character of baptism is most evident when baptism retains its connection with the eucharist in a unified rite of initiation.

I write and speak from the perspective of Roman Catholicism, with its Rite of Christian Initiation for Adults. The rite comprises a process of conversion accompanied by a faith community. The process culminates in a unified rite of initiation including baptism, confirmation, and eucharist at the Easter Vigil, and is followed by a period of instruction in the faith of

1. "On the Councils and the Church."

25

the church. This rite was revised and restored in 1972 in accordance with the mandate of the Second Vatican Council and by decree of Pope Paul VI. The National Conference of Catholic Bishops approved national statutes for the catechumenate in the United States in 1986, and, beginning on September 1, 1988, the Rite of Christian Initiation of Adults was mandated for use whenever an adult or anyone of catechetical age is prepared for baptism. This rite is now normative for our understanding of baptism even though most Roman Catholics are baptized as infants. The norm is established not by the frequency with which a certain form of baptism is administered, but by the form that determines the meaning of baptism.[2] In this case the norm is constituted by the full, conscious, faithful participation in the baptismal rite by an adult. We are still exploring the impact of the rite on the life of the church, on our ecclesiology, and on our understanding of the individual sacraments.

I trust that this material will be relevant to other faith communions even though they may not practice a unified rite of initiation. The model on which it is based, the practice of initiation in the early church, represents a tradition common to all of us. In the years since the Second Vatican Council various Christian communions have grown closer together liturgically with what is largely a common lectionary. Our eucharistic liturgies, though further apart, are showing greater similarities thanks to the historical work being done on the origins and forms of Christian worship that predate our divisions. Following the principle that the law of worship *(lex orandi)* and the law of belief *(lex credendi)* mutually inform each other, I remain convinced that a consideration of our churches' liturgies will help us reflect on our ecclesiologies. In this presentation my thesis is that baptism is an ecclesial sacrament. I refer to a unified rite in my communion in order to support this thesis, but I trust that the trajectory I plan to draw between baptism and the eucharist will be valid for other communions as well.

From the time that we are first catechized, we affirm that through baptism we are reborn in the Spirit, receive sanctifying grace, are freed from sin, become sons and daughters of God and members of Christ's body, are incorporated into the church, and participate in the death and resurrection of Christ. Dangers lurk beneath these familiar answers, however. We can fall into a mechanical notion of grace whereby grace is automatically received when we perform the ritual correctly. Incorporation

2. Aidan Kavanagh, *The Shape of Baptism: The Rite of Christian Initiation* (New York: Pueblo Publishing Co., 1978), pp. 108-9.

and initiation into the church can look as if we've received a membership card into the religious equivalent of a civic organization. Such dangers are particularly acute for those of us who were baptized as infants. How many people experientially affirm that baptism is the most significant event in their life? Those who do are not likely to be Roman Catholics or Lutherans. We are far removed from Tertullian's conviction that "Christians are made, not born."[3]

Baptism does not just incorporate us into the church as a club or an organization. It does not just bestow grace to us as individuals. It makes us "living stones" to be "built into a spiritual house, to be a holy priesthood."[4] Through our participation in the life, death, and resurrection of Christ in baptism we share in his priesthood. Baptism gives us a share in the priesthood of all believers.[5] Just as stones construct a building, so the church is constituted by Christians and is a priestly community by virtue of its being the body of Christ, the high priest. This "house" and this "priesthood" is essentially communal. However, for a number of reasons associated with Christianity becoming a majority rather than minority religion and the disintegration of a unified rite of initiation, the communal meaning of baptism was replaced by a more individualistic focus. This individualistic focus emphasized the salvation of an individual through the removal of sin and the bestowal of grace rather than incorporation into an eschatological community identified as the body of Christ. Eventually, too, the concept of grace became reified, imagined as a quantifiable substance rather than a relationship of communion.

For the early Christians, the implications of baptism were enormous, demanding a total conversion that immediately placed them in a countercultural position at odds with the dominant faith systems, whether Jewish, Roman, or Greek. This conversion was a process that proceeded in stages over what was frequently a three-year period of probation known as the catechumenate. Initiation was not easy, and half-hearted Christians were discouraged from undertaking the process. Since the early sixth century, however, the candidates for baptism have been primarily infants, implying that they are baptized into a Christian culture rather than making an adult personal commitment to personal conversion. Eventually the disintegration of the integral unity of the initiation rites consisting of bap-

---

3. *Apol.* xviii.
4. 1 Peter 2:5.
5. 1 Peter 2:9.

tism, post-baptismal anointing, and eucharist also contributed to the diminishment of awareness of the radical change wrought by baptism.

Today Christianity represents the majority faith tradition in the West. Baptized, believing Christians number more than 1.8 billion people, that is, about one-third of the world population of 5,423,000,000.[6] Christian conversion does not always represent the radical break from a former way of life that it once did, and in many countries baptism is a social and familial event that does not necessarily culminate in a vibrant committed life in the church. Paradoxically, even as Christians represent the majority religion in a geographical area, the experience of baptism becomes more individualized rather than communal as the experience of the church community into which one is baptized becomes more generalized and diffused rather than focused and particular. In other words, our experience of baptism, as contrasted with the theology of baptism, is all too frequently baptism as a moment of our inculturation into a dominant culture, rather than a conversion and entrance into a particular faith community. Perhaps one can argue that the dominant culture constitutes a faith community of Christians, but this is not convincing if the conversion to Christianity does not entail a critique of non-Christian values operative within that culture.

Disintegration of a Unified Rite of Initiation

In the baptismal rites of the third century recounted for us in the *Apostolic Tradition,* generally attributed to Hippolytus (d. 215), baptism clearly culminates in the eucharist. After their baptism the neophytes join the faithful in their prayers and to exchange the kiss of peace with them. Then the eucharist begins and the newly baptized celebrate their incorporation into the body of Christ by sharing in eucharistic communion. The eucharist is the climax of their process of conversion, and they are admitted to it only after perhaps as much as three years of association with the church.

Mark Searle describes the break-up of Christian initiation in the sixth century and attributes it largely to the fact that the candidates for baptism were almost exclusively infants. Because of the high infant mortality and the widely accepted doctrine of Augustine on original sin, the preoccupation shifted from forming Christians for life to saving children

6. Joseph F. Eagan, *Restoration and Renewal: The Church in the Third Millennium* (Kansas City: Sheed and Ward, 1995), p. 6.

from dying unbaptized.[7] This resulted in the gradual abandonment of Easter and Pentecost as the annual festivals of initiation, although the unified rite of initiation survived in Rome, with the exception of the danger of death, until the twelfth century.[8] The removal of baptism from the season of Easter resulted in the abbreviation of the preparatory rites and in all the rites of initiation eventually being condensed into a single ceremony. Secondly, baptism was no longer celebrated by the bishop and the whole church, but by a priest and whoever wanted to attend. In the East bishops delegated priests to carry out the full rites of initiation including baptism, post-baptismal anointing with oil consecrated by the bishop, and eucharistic communion. In the West the infant was baptized by a priest and then taken to the bishop at some later time for a chrismation that later came to be known as "confirmation." In the sixteenth century the Council of Trent decreed that a child should not be confirmed until the age of reason, generally reckoned to be about seven years of age. This displacement of confirmation figures largely in any discussion of the disintegration of the rites of initiation, but since this sacrament is not the focus of this chapter, I will not pursue this topic in any further detail.[9]

7. Mark Searle, *Christening: The Making of Christians* (Collegeville, Minn.: Liturgical Press, 1980), p. 14.

8. Maxwell Johnson drew my attention to recent scholarship questioning the assumed normativity of Easter as the occasion for baptism as well as a Romans 6 paschal theology for interpreting Christian initiation in the early church. See Gabriele Winkler, "Das armenische Initiationsrituale," *Orientalia Christiana Analecta* 217 (Rome, 1982), and "Die Licht-Ersheinung bei der Taufe Jesu und der Ursprung des Epiphaniefestes," *Oriens Christianus* 78 (1994): 177-229; Thomas Tally, *The Origins of the Liturgical Year*, 2nd edition (Collegeville, Minn.: Liturgical Press, 1986); Paul Bradshaw, "'*Diem baptismo sollemniorem*': Initiation and Easter in Christian Antiquity," in Johnson (ed.), *Living Water, Sealing Spirit: Readings on Christian Initiation* (Collegeville: Liturgical Press/Pueblo, 1995), pp. 137-47; Maxwell Johnson, "From Three Weeks to Forty Days: Baptismal Preparation and the Origins of Lent," in the same volume, pp. 88-136; Maxwell Johnson, "Preparation for Pascha? The Origins of Lent in Christian Antiquity," in Paul Bradshaw and Lawrence Hoffman (eds.), *Two Liturgical Traditions*, vol. 5: *Passover and Easter* (Notre Dame: University of Notre Dame Press, forthcoming).

9. See Canon J. D. C. Fischer, *Christian Initiation: Baptism in the Medieval West*, Alcuin Club Collections 47 (London: S.P.C.K., 1965); L. L. Mitchell, *Baptismal Anointing*, Alcuin Club Collections 48 (London: S.P.C.K., 1966); A. P. Milner, *The Theology of Confirmation*, Theology Today Series 26 (Notre Dame, Ind.: Fides Publishers, 1971); Nathan Mitchell, "Dissolution of the Rite of Christian Initiation," in *Made, Not Born: New Perspectives on Christian Initiation and the Catechumenate* (Notre Dame: University of Notre Dame Press, 1976), pp. 50-82.

Although confirmation became detached from the rest of the initiation process, children in the West continued to be admitted to communion at their baptism. Fischer reports that "in all the Churches of the West those who were granted Paschal initiation, whether or not they then received confirmation, were all, irrespective of age, communicated at the Mass which formed the climax of the rite."[10] Once the eucharist had been received, another reception of the sacrament could be deferred for a long time, but there was great emphasis that the eucharist should be received before death. In this context, it is not a question of receiving the eucharist before imminent death; the emphasis is on a person having received the eucharist at all, including infants. The Scripture text of John 6:53, "Very truly, I tell you, unless you eat the flesh of the Son of Man and drink his blood, you have no life in you," seemed to mandate the reception of communion for all."[11]

This changed in the twelfth century following eucharistic controversies and an emphasis on sacramental realism, which raised doubts about whether infants should be communed with eucharistic bread since they would be unable to swallow the host. Even though communing them with eucharistic wine remained a possibility, the chalice was soon withdrawn from the laity — with the effect of excommunicating children. The general rule was then that they could not be admitted until they reached "years of discretion."[12] The Fourth Lateran Council (1215) imposed the discipline of going to confession and receiving the eucharist at Easter on those faithful who had reached the age of discretion.[13] In 1562 the Council of Trent decreed that children under the age of discernment are not bound by any obligation to sacramental holy communion.[14] When Pius X lowered the age for the reception of communion in 1910, but not for confirmation, the sequence for the rites of initiation became baptism-penance-eucharist-confirmation. Within this sequence, eucharist is not experienced as the culmination of initiation regardless of whatever theologies might be in place.

10. Fischer, p. 101.

11. Fischer, p. 103.

12. This history of infant communion in the West is described by Paul Bradshaw in "Christian Initiation," *The New Dictionary of Sacramental Worship* (Collegeville, Minn.: Liturgical Press, 1990), p. 606.

13. Fourth Lateran Council, c. 21.

14. Session 21, 16 July 1562, chap. 4, canon 4.

Effects of the Loss of an Integrated Rite

Numerous effects followed the disintegration of the unity of the rites of initiation. Christian initiation ceased to be a process and became a series of three separate rites. Not only have these rites been separated, but the order of their reception has been changed. Today children are usually admitted to communion before they are confirmed, and Roman Catholic sacramental legislation prescribes that they receive first penance before their first communion. The separation and the reordering destroy the direct trajectory from baptism to eucharist, although a eucharistic doctrine that loses its connection with the mystical body of Christ, that is, its ecclesial meaning, and becomes solely associated with an individual's reception of the sacramental body of Christ is also to blame.[15] Within our faith traditions we are very clear that we receive the body of Christ when we receive the eucharist, but how conscious are we that we also sacramentalize our communion with one another within the church which is the mystical body of Christ? We've largely lost the ecclesial meaning of the eucharist. Some who try to restore it may be accused of a certain horizontalism in their eucharistic piety, implying that the transcendent nature of the eucharist has been lost. Such criticisms, however, fail to acknowledge that the ecclesial meaning of the eucharist is rooted in the identity of the ecclesial community as the body of Christ within the Pauline theology of 1 Corinthians 10:16-17.

Initiation also became privatized and isolated from the faith community. Most often, baptisms were celebrated Sunday afternoon with only the family in attendance. The emphasis on the removal of original sin eclipsed its formational function of "making a Christian" and incorporating that person into the Christian community. Only a remnant of the community was even present to receive and welcome the new member.

One result of this privatization is that baptism came to be seen more as a "mark of an individual Christian" than a "mark of the church." Roman Catholic theology does speak of baptism along with two other unrepeatable sacraments, confirmation and orders, as conferring a sacramental character metaphorically described as an indelible spiritual "mark." Interestingly, this "mark," described as an "indelible mark on the soul," was also susceptible to individualistic interpretations.[16] This "mark" is a configura-

15. Henri de Lubac traces this separation in *Corpus Mysticum: L'Euchariste et l'Eglise au Moyen Age*, Coll. Théologie 3 (Paris: Aubier-Montaigne, 1944).

16. The Council of Florence (1438-45), The Council of Trent (1545-63), canons on

tion to Christ, a belonging to Christ, which no sin can erase. Its indelible quality is not because of any human capability, but because of the faithfulness of Christ. In baptism we do not claim Christ as much as Christ claims us, and he does so irrevocably.

A Priestly Community

The sacramental character or "mark" also places us in relationship to the church. It is an ordination in the sense that it give us our place within the church.[17] Baptism orders us within a priestly community, confirmation orders us within a prophetic community, and the sacrament of orders bestows the ability to represent the church and Christ in the governance and sacramental life of the church. What is significant is that all these sacraments place us within a network of relationships. The church is the locus of intersection of these relationships. Another way of saying this is that the church is the locus of charisms, since baptism and confirmation in their bestowal of the Spirit confer gifts for the building up of the body that are personal and particular to each individual, yet oriented to the good of the community. The community, then, is "marked" with these gifts as a kingly, prophetic, and priestly community in its identity as the body of Christ who was priest, prophet, and king.

Baptism marks the church as a priestly community because it identifies us with Christ through our immersion into his death and resurrection within the baptismal waters. The gospels never call Christ priest or say that he offered himself in sacrifice. For that matter, neither does Paul. The Letter to the Hebrews alone calls Christ "priest" and "high priest" and describes his work in priestly terms. According to this letter, Christ offered

---

the Sacraments in General, c. 9. However, the *Catechism of the Catholic Church* makes clear that the sacramental character or "seal" is related to Christ's priesthood and that it remains forever in the Christian as a "vocation to divine worship and to the service of the Church" (698, 1121).

17. In the theology of Thomas Aquinas, baptism is a relational act that places a person in community with Christ, the head of the ecclesial body, and with the gathered assembly. See *Summa Theologiae*, IIIa, 63, 1; *Summa Theologiae*, IIIa, 70, 1; and *Summa Theologiae*, IIIa, 63, 1. For a discussion of baptism as an ordination see John D. Zizioulas, *Being As Communion* (Crestwood, New York: St. Vladimir's Press, 1985), pp. 215ff. Edward Schillebeeckx also describes character as an ordination in *Christ the Sacrament of the Encounter with God* (Kansas City: Sheed and Ward, 1963), p. 167.

himself as victim (Heb. 7:27; 9:14, 25). Christ's sacrifice was the doing of God's will, the offering of his personal obedience unto death (10:5-10). If the doing of God's will unites himself perfectly with God, on the other hand, taking on the death of sinners unites Christ with human beings.[18] The result is that Christians have the same access to God that Christ had. Christians, too, are invited to offer the sacrifice of their own lives. For example in Romans, Paul says, "I appeal to you therefore, brothers and sisters, by the mercies of God, to present your bodies as a living sacrifice, holy and acceptable to God, which is your spiritual worship. Do not be conformed to this world, but be transformed by the renewing of your minds, so that you may discern what is the will of God — what is good and acceptable and perfect" (Rom. 12:1-2). The priesthood of Christians is possible because of Christ's priesthood and his relationship of solidarity with us.

Individual Christians, lay or ordained, do not have a priestly role apart from the priestly community which is the church. The church is priestly because it is the mystical body of Christ who was the high priest. The priestly character of the church community is most evident in its worship of the Father in the celebration of the eucharist, the source and summit of the church's activity, and the culmination of Christian initiation. In baptism, through our union with Christ the high priest, we participate in the same service which Christ rendered to the Father in his suffering, death, and resurrection. In the words of Schillebeeckx, "a baptized member of the Church receives the commission and therefore the competence, duty and right to take an active part in the ecclesial mystery of Easter. This activity is primarily the sacramental activity of the Church, above all in the eucharist, in which the mystery of Easter is realized in the fullest sense."[19]

Even though a baptized person who has not communicated is not less a member of the church, we recognize that something in that person's baptism has not been brought to visible, sacramental expression in the absence of the eucharist. Baptism constitutes the baptized as a "liturgical person" oriented to worship in the official prayer of the church which is both public and paschal. That person has been incorporated into a priestly community by baptism, but without the eucharist, the priestly *exercise* of that community is missing, at least with respect to its highest expression.

18. See Albert Vanhoye, "Sacerdoce commun et sacerdoce ministériel: distinction et rapports," *Nouvelle revue théologique* 97 (1975): 193-207.

19. Schillebeeckx, p. 163.

The eucharist is the visible, sacramental sign of all the baptized in communion in the body of Christ within a concrete community that experiences its identity as the body of Christ. The Christian's relationship to Christ is inseparable from that person's relationship to the corporate body, the church. We are baptized into both Christ and the church. What happens in baptism is not the bestowal of reified grace, but the insertion of a person into a network of relationships which in theological terms we describe as a "communion." That very state of being-in-communion with Father, Son, and Spirit is what constitutes grace and salvation. Furthermore, we are in communion with the Triune God in the company of one another.

The Rite of Christian Initiation of Adults, in the instruction for the celebration of the sacraments of initiation, describes the activities of the priesthood of the baptized. These include the right to join the community in common prayer, have a part in the general intercessions, bring gifts to the altar, exchange the sign of peace, share in the offering of the sacrifice, express the spirit of adoption as God's children which they have received in baptism through the recitation of the Lord's Prayer, and commune in the eucharist.[20] These activities are symbols of full membership in the church and exercises of the priestly identity of the church.

There is a mutual reciprocity between the nature of the church as a liturgical, priestly community, and the liturgy as the work of the priestly community. This is evident in both a document on the nature of the church and a document on the liturgy from the Second Vatican Council. According to the Dogmatic Constitution on the Church, "the faithful are appointed by their baptismal character to Christian religious worship" (11). Here the nature of the community leads to worship. That same council's Constitution on the Sacred Liturgy states: "It is very much the wish of the church that all the faithful should be led to take that full, conscious and active part in liturgical celebrations which is demanded by the very nature of the liturgy, and to which the Christian people, 'a chosen race, a royal priesthood, a holy nation, a redeemed people' (1 Pet. 2:9, 4-5) have a right and to which they are bound by reason of their Baptism" (14). Here the liturgy defines the nature of the community.

---

20. *The Rites of the Catholic Church*, vol. 1 (New York: Pueblo Publishing Co., 1990), #217.

The Rite of Christian Initiation of Adults: Reintegration of Baptism and Eucharist

Just as the Rite of Christian Initiation makes adult baptism at the Easter vigil the norm for understanding baptism, the eucharist at the Easter vigil is where the eucharist is most itself in public and the "standard that defines the meaning of everything else — cross and sacrifice, memorial and presence, ministry and priesthood, intercession and prayer, participation and communion."[21] The eucharist is the culmination of initiation because it is there that the communion of believers with one another and with Christ is sacramentally visible in the sacrament of God's presence with us. With its associations with the messianic banquet, it is a sign of the ultimate and final union to which we are called and which will be completed only in the eschatological end time.

Aidan Kavanagh eloquently describes the relationship between baptism and the eucharist when he articulates the principle on which the rite's norm of baptism rests:

> that baptism is inadequately perceptible apart from the eucharist; that the eucharist is not wholly knowable without reference to conversion in faith; that conversion is abortive if it does not issue in sacramental illumination by incorporation into the Church; that the Church is only an inept corporation without steady access to Sunday, Lent, and the Easter Vigil; that evangelization is mere noise and catechesis only a syllabus apart from conversion and initiation into a robust ecclesial environment of faith shared. In baptism the eucharist begins, and in the eucharist baptism is sustained. From this premier sacramental union flows all the Church's life.[22]

An examination of the Rite of Christian Initiation of Adults reveals its nature as an ecclesial event. At the beginning of the rite of acceptance into the Order of Catechumens, the candidates are asked: "What do you ask of God's Church?"[23] In the second step, the rite of election or enrollment of names, the church judges the readiness of the catechumens to advance toward the sacraments of initiation on the basis of the testimony of

---

21. Nathan D. Mitchell, *Forum Essays: Eucharist as Sacrament of Initiation* (Chicago: Liturgy Training Publications, 1994), pp. 109-10.

22. Kavanagh, p. 122.

23. *Rite of Christian Initiation of Adults*, p. 51.

godparents and catechists. The church then elects them, an eloquent indication that baptism is not something we undertake entirely of our own initiative or alone.[24] The rite instructs that before the rite of election

> the bishop, priests, deacons, catechists, godparents, and the entire community, in accord with their respective responsibilities and in their own way, should, after considering the matter carefully, arrive at a judgment about the catechumens' state of formation and progress. After the election, they should surround the elect with prayer, so that the entire Church will accompany and lead them to encounter Christ.[25]

Within the rite of election itself, the bishop celebrant or his delegate declares in the presence of the community the church's approval of the candidates.[26] Also within this rite the catechumens affirm their desire "to enter fully into the life of the Church through the sacraments of baptism, confirmation, and the eucharist,"[27] indicating that these sacraments of initiation are gates into the life of the church.

The ecclesial dimension of baptism is associated with the conviction that all who are baptized into Christ have become one in Christ Jesus (Gal. 3:27-28). This unity in Christ is expressed by Paul in the image of the body: "For just as the body is one and has many members, and all the members of the body, though many, are one body, so it is with Christ. For in the one Spirit we were all baptized into one body — Jews or Greeks, slaves or free — and we were all made to drink of one Spirit" (1 Cor. 12:12-13). By being baptized into the death and resurrection of Christ we become his body, not individually, although there is a transformation in grace whereby we are transformed into the likeness of Christ, but corporately.

Here the trajectory between baptism and eucharist, the sacrament of Christ's body and blood, is evident. They are both sacraments of the same body and we participate in the body through different sacramental modalities. Just as Christ is sacramentalized on the altar, so is the church. The communion into which we are baptized, both Christic and ecclesial, is represented by the sacrament of the altar. In terms of sacramental symbolism, the water bath symbolizes our immersion in the death and resurrection of Christ and the eucharist represents our communion in Christ. The eucha-

---

24. *The Rites*, #119.
25. *The Rites*, #121.
26. *The Rites*, #122.
27. *The Rites*, #132.

rist is the repeatable communal form of the incorporation into Christ achieved under different sacramental signs in baptism.

Aside from the eucharist's position as the ritual completion of initiation within the RCIA, there are a number of theological reasons for the direct link between baptism and eucharist. First, both sacraments sacramentalize an individual's participation in the paschal mystery. Second, both sacraments sacramentalize an individual's communion in the church. These are not simply separate and discrete moments. They are integrally related because the church is the body of Christ. The church itself is a sacrament of the paschal mystery since it is the sacrament of Christ in an analogous use of the category of sacrament.[28]

According to the introduction to the Rite of Christian Initiation of Adults, the whole initiation bears a "markedly paschal character, since the initiation of Christians is the first sacramental sharing in Christ's dying and rising and since, in addition, the period of purification and enlightenment ordinarily coincide with Lent and the period of postbaptismal catechesis or mystagogy with the Easter season."[29] Thus both the content of the rite and the time of the rite are paschal. In the words of Jean Daniélou, "The Christian faith has only one object, the mystery of Christ dead and risen."[30] This one mystery subsists under both the sacramental mode of baptism and the sacramental mode of eucharist. In baptism the sacramental sign is immersion into the death and resurrection of Christ in the waters of baptism. In the eucharist the sign is the body and blood of Christ crucified and risen.

The Rite of Christian Initiation makes it clear that baptism is an ecclesial event and that there are a number of ecclesial effects of the rite.[31] First, initiation into the church is a public rather than a private process. There are a number of steps that take place before the assembled community: making their intention known before the community and being enrolled in the catechumenate, the "election" to enter proximate preparation

---

28. See Schillebeeckx, *Christ the Sacrament of the Encounter with God* and Karl Rahner, *The Church and the Sacraments* (Freiburg: Herder, 1963).

29. *The Rites*, #8.

30. "Le symbolisme des rites baptismaux," *Dieu Vivant* 1 (1945). Translation by Robert Taft, S.J. And cited in Robert Taft, S.J., *Beyond East and West: Problems in Liturgical Understanding* (Washington, D.C.: The Pastoral Press, 1984), p. 11.

31. Margaret Mary Kelleher, O.S.B., enumerates these in "Ecclesial Nature of Baptism," in *The New Dictionary of Sacramental Worship*, ed. Peter E. Fink, S.J. (Collegeville, Minn.: A Michael Glazier Book, Liturgical Press, 1990), p. 87.

for the sacraments of initiation, the scrutinies and exorcisms after the homily at the main eucharistic celebrations on the third, fourth, and fifth Sundays in Lent, and the reception of baptism, confirmation, and eucharist at the Easter vigil. The formal rituals before the assembly are supported by the relationships forged outside of times of formal worship. In the mid-second-century text, the *First Apology* of Justin Martyr, those preparing for baptism were expected to pray and fast and ask forgiveness of sin. However, Justin Martyr adds that the community were to pray and fast with them.[32] Thus there was community solidarity with the catechumens in their process of initiation.

Second, the growth in faith required of the catechumen is not merely intellectual assent to the doctrines of the church. The faith required is a commitment to paschal living, which entails a radical transformation of life and values to be lived publicly. Thus the RCIA entails a shift from an educational, "inquiry" model of initiation to one that emphasizes conversion. This conversion takes place within and is molded by the liturgy, the public prayer of the church — specifically by a lectionary catechesis. It also occurs in communion with a particular faith community, which ideally models lives of conversion. Catechumens learn what it means to be a Christian by observing this in the concrete lives of others.

Third, the rite requires a vibrant church community into which the catechumen can be initiated. There is a reciprocal cycle: the catechumen is initiated into a vibrant community which is in turn made more vibrant because of the addition of a committed, converted member. However, at some point we need to enter the circle. The revised process of initiation contributes to the vitality of a faith community, but we need to examine other aspects of our community life which contribute to that vitality: liturgy, social activities, social justice outreach, education, etc. Faith comes to expression in all these activities. The RCIA initiates a cycle whereby faith is brought to articulation, and this articulation in turn increases faith which in turn seeks expression in various ecclesial activities. This is as true for the neophyte as for the congregation. In short, the process of initiation presupposes an ecclesiology of the church as a committed, converted people of God and in turn contributes to such an ecclesiology.

32. Justin Martyr, *First Apology*, 61.

The Ecumenical Dimension

The direct trajectory between baptism and eucharist which the Rite of Christian Initiation elucidates poses anew questions raised by the common recognition of baptism accompanied by the refusal of admission to a common eucharist. It is generally recognized that baptism constitutes the unity acknowledged among Christians. When administered with water in the name of the Triune God we affirm that there is but one baptism — despite the existence of many confessional communions — in the affirmation of Ephesians 4:4 that "there is one body and one Spirit, just as you were called to the one hope of your calling, one Lord, one faith, one baptism, one God and Father of all." Likewise, in Paul's first letter to the Corinthians baptism appears as a ritual sign of Christian unity: "Is Christ divided? Was Paul crucified for you? Or were you baptized in the name of Paul?" (1 Cor. 1:13). And: "By one Spirit we were all baptized into one body . . . and all were made to drink of one Spirit" (1 Cor. 12:13).

The unity of Christians in this one baptism is affirmed in the document, *Baptism, Eucharist and Ministry:*

> Administered in obedience to our Lord, baptism is a sign and seal of our common discipleship. Through baptism, Christians are brought into union with Christ, with each other, and with the Church of every time and place. Our common baptism, which unites us to Christ in faith, is thus a basic bond of unity. We are one people and are called to confess and serve one Lord in each place and in all the world. The union with Christ which we share through baptism has important implications for Christian unity. . . . When baptismal unity is realized in one holy, catholic, apostolic Church, a genuine Christian witness can be made to the healing and reconciling love of God. Therefore, our one baptism into Christ constitutes a call to the churches to overcome their divisions and visibly manifest their fellowship.[33]

The scandal of Christianity is that groups separated from one another celebrate the "ritual sign of a christologically, soteriologically and pneumatologically grounded unity."[34] How can this be? The Second Vati-

---

33. *Baptism, Eucharist and Ministry,* Faith and Order Paper No. 111 (Geneva: World Council of Churches, 1982), #6.

34. Geoffrey Wainwright, *Doxology: The Praise of God in Worship, Doctrine, and Life* (New York: Oxford University Press, 1980), p. 123.

can Council's Decree on Ecumenism provides a clue. The primary baptismal text in the document is found in #22, which takes up the baptismal theology of Romans 6:4 and Colossians 2:12 and speaks of baptism as incorporation into the crucified and glorified Christ and as constituting the sacramental bond of unity existing among all who through it are reborn. The text notes, however, that baptism is only a beginning, an inauguration: "Baptism, therefore, is oriented towards the complete profession of faith, complete incorporation into the institution of salvation such as Christ willed it to be, and finally the completeness of unity which eucharistic communion gives." One can deduce from the text that unity is not found absolutely in baptism since the unity achieved is only an "imperfect" one and baptism is only a "point of departure" for full unity. In other words, baptism is only one of the criteria for church unity. This conciliar text is important because, although it clearly states that baptism constitutes the sacramental bond of unity among the baptized, it distinguishes between imperfect and perfect communion and speaks of a communion created by baptism, then characterizes the communion among Christians who participate in the one baptism as imperfect.

The unity achieved in baptism is a soteriological unity in Christ. We experience unity, but this is an invisible unity in grace. What baptism is ordered toward but cannot contain within itself belongs to the visible elements of unity. If the Decree on Ecumenism states that the unity achieved in baptism is partial, this is not because the mystery represented by baptism is partial or that our incorporation into Christ and the church in baptism is partial, but because such an incorporation requires visible expression within a eucharistic community. The eucharist is the repeated and ongoing sacrament of the incorporation into the body of Christ achieved in baptism. The unity we achieve in baptism is incomplete because we are unable to share in the same eucharist. The reason for this lies in the relationship between eucharistic communities.

The question is: Into what church are we baptized, the universal church of Christ or a particular, local church? Here, again, the answer is that we are baptized into both and that there is a relationship of mutual interiority between the two. The universal church only has existence in and through particular churches. In the language of the Dogmatic Constitution on the Church, the universal church subsists in the particular churches. However, most concretely, we are baptized into a worshiping assembly. For Lutherans this worshiping assembly is the basic unit of the church, while for Roman Catholics the basic unit is the particular church defined as an altar community around its bishops. However, the principle of baptism into a basic unit of the church which is fundamentally eucharistic remains the same for both confessions. The irony is that we are baptized into unity and disunity simultaneously — unity because of our unity of one baptism in Christ, disunity because we are baptized into a particular community that is not in communion with other communities.

The altar communities into which we are baptized are not in union with one another. Historically, communion ecclesiology was the first ecclesiology in the church. The church was conceptualized as a communion of communions. *Communio* represented both the unity between the faithful and the bishop as well as the unity between the local churches, represented by the unity of the bishops with one another.[35] This *communio* was realized and represented in eucharistic communion. This does not mean that the communion here is not the soteriological communion of participation in Christ. It does mean, however, that eucharistic communion includes the visible communion of union with a bishop and also the union of local churches with each other through the *communio* of the bishops. Bishops excommunicated each other, and the church of the excommunicated bishop was then out of communion with the other local churches.

The practice of the exchange of communion letters illustrates the relationship. If a person was in communion with a bishop and presented a letter to that effect to another bishop, that person would be admitted to communion if the two bishops were in communion. The participants in the synod at which Paul of Samosata was excommunicated in 268 wrote to the bishops of Rome and Alexandria, requesting that they write to the new bishop and receive communion letters from him.[36]

The theology and practice of early communion ecclesiology indicates that eucharistic communion, somewhat unlike baptismal communion, is strongly associated with visible ecclesial structures and ministry. While both baptism and eucharist signify both communion in the dead and risen Christ, and communion in a church, baptism effects entrance into a concrete and specific faith community that has structures and ministry which put it into communion with other faith communities or which

---

35. In the ecclesiology of Vatican II the communion of particular churches is sacramentalized in the college of bishops, the union of bishops representing in their person the union of churches. See Susan Wood, "The Sacramentality of Episcopal Consecration," *Theological Studies* 51 (1990): 479-96.

36. Eusebius, *Church History* 7.30.17.

dissociate it from those groups.[37] The emphasis on the local church within communion ecclesiology both allows us to appreciate the diversity of various communions and to envision ecumenical unity as a communion of communions, but it also points to the difficulties of communion and how those are tied to ecclesial structures. The profound unity achieved in baptism does not automatically result in the mutual reception of other ecclesial communities into eucharistic communion. What is lacking is not necessarily of the soteriological order, but of the order of mutual recognition of other communities. The emphasis on the visible structures of unity was a way of assuring the unity of faith among the various communities.

The eucharist profoundly embodies ecclesial symbolism. It represents the unity of the baptized in the body of Christ and the communion of churches. This, however, is not what is usually experienced in the pain occasioned by the absence of eucharistic hospitality between our churches. Even though we are baptized into specific concrete faith communities, our experience is not usually one of asking to be admitted to communion with another local community. More frequently our sense of universal communion in Christ wins over our sense of locality.

The completion that the eucharist brings to baptism is twofold: first, the visible, ongoing sacramental communion in the body of Christ, the same body in which we already participate in baptism, and, second, the visible communion both with a local church and, through the local church, with the other eucharistic communions. Not to be able to concretize or sacramentalize the unity we share in baptism around a common eucharistic table represents an incongruency and self-contradiction.

When baptism and eucharist are seen as a continuous trajectory — baptism being completed, made visible, sacramentalized, as it were, in the eucharist — they reciprocally interpret each other. We are baptized into a eucharistic community, and, conversely, the eucharistic community is the community of the baptized. Through baptism we are formed into a priestly people and by the baptismal character are given a place in the eucharistic worship of the Christian community. We are baptized into the eucharist. The eucharist is the ongoing sacramental realization of the in-

---

37. *The Church Local and Universal* states this principle thus: "Communion . . . refers to a dynamic, spiritual, objective reality which is embodied in ecclesial structures. The gift of communion from God is not an amorphous reality but an organic unity that requires a canonical form of expression. The purpose of such canonical structuring is to ensure that the local churches (and their members), in their communion with each together, can live in harmony and fidelity to 'the faith which has been once and for all entrusted to the saints' " (Jude 3).

corporation in Christ and the church accomplished in baptism. A eucharistic spirituality is also a baptismal spirituality. Theologies of baptism and the eucharist, when developed independently of each other, fail to show their interrelationship. When we recover the trajectory between these two sacraments, perhaps through an integrated rite of initiation, the spirituality of the eucharist will retrieve its baptismal basis. Then the asymmetry between a universal baptism and a confession-bound eucharist will become even more uneven. To continue to recognize one sacrament and not the other breaks the essential unity of the rite of initiation. Then the tragedy of our disunion will become even clearer.

Baptism and the Church's Faith

JOHN H. ERICKSON

In the Niceo-Constantinopolitan Creed we say, "I believe — *pisteuo*, I have faith — in one God, the Father almighty, maker of heaven and earth and of all things visible and invisible; and in one Lord, Jesus Christ. . . ." Statements follow about who Jesus Christ is and what he has done "for us and for our salvation." Thereafter we continue, "And in the Holy Spirit, the Lord, the giver of life, who proceeds from the Father, who with the Father and the Son together is worshiped and glorified, who spoke by the prophets. And in one holy, catholic and apostolic Church. I confess one baptism for the remission of sins. I await the resurrection of the dead, and the life of the world to come."

I would like to concentrate on these last affirmations of the creed, which speak of the Holy Spirit, the one church and the one baptism for the remission of sins, with some reference also to the awaited resurrection. These affirmations are not in close conjunction simply because they could not be fitted in neatly elsewhere in the creed. They can be found in close conjunction not only in Niceo-Constantinopolitan but also in other early Christian creeds. For example, in what is perhaps the oldest, the Old Roman baptismal symbol commonly known as the Apostles' Creed, we say: "And in the Holy Spirit, the holy Church, the remission of sins, the resurrection of the flesh." There is an intimate connection between these affirmations, and also between them and the word that introduces the whole creed, *pisteuo:* "I believe," "I have faith."

Let us consider first what is meant by *faith.* Here it is commonplace to distinguish between an objective aspect and a subjective aspect, between "that which is believed" and "that by which we believe," between faith un-

44

derstood in conceptual terms and faith understood in personalist terms, faith understood as certain improbable propositions that are objectively true and faith understood as assent to such propositions on the part of individuals who find them in some way meaningful for their personal lives. But whether faith is understood primarily in objective terms or in subjective terms, we tend to take for granted that it is something characteristic of religious people. We say "so-and-so is a person of great faith," by this meaning that "so-and-so holds strong religious convictions," whatever these may be.

In fact, faith is not unique to religious people. In a very stimulating article on "Faith and Sacraments in the Conversion Process," Mark Searle, a Catholic liturgiologist, sketches the work that has been done on this subject by developmental psychologists.[1] He points to the work of James Fowler, for example, who describes faith as a "human universal." According to Fowler, faith designates "a way of leaning into life . . . a way of making sense of one's existence. It denotes a way of giving order and coherence to the force-field of life. It speaks of the investment of life-grounding trust and of life-orienting commitment."[2] The point behind these impressive words is clear. As Searle observes, "Thus understood, faith is the basis of every human life."[3] No one lives without faith, without some way of "leaning into life." Taken in this sense, faith is a deep-seated reality that precedes self-conscious reflection and articulation in propositional form. It therefore may never fully come to the surface or be brought to full consciousness. We may become aware of the faith by which we live only at a moment of crisis or confrontation, when our usual routines of life break down. But even when faith is not fully articulated, as Searle notes, "it underlies all we say and do and manifests itself in our habitual actions and reactions." It is "embodied in our life and lifestyle before it 'comes to mind,'" before we even begin to reflect on our life and lifestyle.[4]

There is nothing specifically religious about faith thus understood, much less specifically Christian. While it is hard to imagine anyone living completely without faith, it is very easy to imagine someone living without Christian faith, leaning on any number of false gods. Who or what is it that

1. Searle, "Faith and Sacraments in the Conversion Process," in *Conversion and the Catechumenate,* ed. Robert Duggan (New York: Paulist, 1984), pp. 64-84.
2. "Perspectives on the Family from the Standpoint of Faith Development Theory," *Perkins Journal* (Fall 1979): 7, as quoted by Searle, p. 66.
3. Searle, p. 66.
4. Searle, p. 66.

gives meaning and direction to our life and receives our commitment? In antiquity there were many false gods. One of the most pervasive forms of idolatry was expressed in emperor-worship; behind this stood the idea that the Greco-Roman way of life, with its maintenance of "law and order," was an ultimate good. In our own day there also are many false gods. Consider what the media have to say. "Buick is something to believe in." "GE brings good things to life." "Levis 501s — the buttons shall set you free." "Love is Musk."[5] Often our way of "leaning into life" is formed by such notions. Our gods become financial security or status or power or successful personal relationships, often sexual in nature. How does one move — or how is one moved — from faith in such gods to Christian faith? In antiquity, how did one move from the culture of death that was epitomized in the gladiatorial arena and the fatalism of the various philosophies of the day to Christian faith, with its horizon of hope ("I await the resurrection of the dead") and its affirmation of the Holy Spirit as "giver of life"? How did one move from the worship of the emperor and his global empire to the confession of *"one Lord,* Jesus Christ" and "the Holy Spirit, the *Lord"?* How did one move from the various dualistic cults that preached liberation of the invisible inner self from this visible world of meaninglessness to belief in *"one* God, the Father almighty, maker of heaven and earth, and of all things visible and invisible"? In our own day we have many of the same questions. In a world that lives by conspicuous consumption, where aggressiveness and competition are highly prized characteristics, where the only alternative seems to be death through mass suicide or drugs, can we really believe in the Lordship of someone who preached humility, poverty, responsible concern for creation, and love for enemies?

For an answer to such questions, we must consider more closely what is meant by another word, baptism. Baptism has been described as a "concertina" word: its definition expands and contracts like an accordion.[6] Sometimes the word baptism is used in a narrow sense to refer to a triple encounter with water accompanied by invocation of the name of the Father and of the Son and of the Holy Spirit. But baptism also has a broader meaning, making it practically synonymous with Christian initiation. For

5. Some of these illustrations as well as others are given by James B. Dunning, "Confronting the Demons: The Social Dimensions of Conversion," in *Conversion and the Catechumenate,* p. 27.

6. James Dunn, *Baptism in the Holy Spirit* (= Studies in Biblical Theology, second series, 15; London: SCM, 1970), p. 5.

Orthodox Christians, the "sacrament of baptism" (understood in the narrow sense) is followed immediately by the "sacrament of chrismation" and relatively quickly by reception of the eucharist. For this reason we Orthodox Christians like to call attention to the fact that, unlike most Western Christians, we have preserved the unitary character of Christian initiation. But our understanding of Christian initiation — that is, baptism in its wider sense — should not be limited simply to these three particularly solemn and conspicuous "sacraments." For early Christians baptism was a process of conversion. It began with first enrollment as a catechumen. It extended through a longer or shorter period of instruction in the truths of the Christian faith and of practice in Christian living. It included exorcism of demons and rejection of false gods, making it a total reorientation of life and values. This process reached a climactic moment in baptism in the narrow sense, when the baptizand made the church's faith his own, when in response to questions posed to him at the baptismal pool he was able to say "*I* believe . . ." (And here we should keep in mind that creeds like the Old Roman and the Niceo-Constantinopolitan were not originally freestanding, self-sufficient statements of the church's faith; they had their origin precisely in the responses the baptizand made at the moment of baptism.) This process continued as the baptizand exchanged the sacred kiss of peace with his fathers, brothers, and sisters in Christ and joined them in eucharistic fellowship. But even there it did not stop. Deepening of Christian faith continued through post-baptismal mystagogy and was renewed in reception of the eucharist, in prayer, in ascetical struggle, so that the baptizand's whole life reflected his faith — the church's faith — in God's saving power.

All this we have heard before. But let us beware of certain misconceptions that can easily arise when we consider baptism in this wider sense. Even when we use terms like "Christian initiation" and "process" when referring to baptism in order to underscore its unitary and dynamic character, we still tend to divide this process into distinct, discrete moments that proceed in a linear and sequential way and whose meaning can be analyzed at each point: first this, then that. We Orthodox Christians sometimes congratulate ourselves that, unlike Western Christians, we do not separate these moments temporally, but in formal presentations of sacramental theology we do tend to separate them conceptually. We adopt a linear and analytical approach that in fact is quite at odds with the circular and contemplative approach which over the centuries has characterized the Christian East. In approaching theological issues, representative figures like St. Maximus the Confessor and St. Gregory Palamas introduce one aspect of the mystery under consideration, often in the form of pithy maxims drawn from the fathers who went before them, and then, without fully developing it, they move on to other aspects, only to return to the initial aspect at a later point, from a slightly different and often higher perspective. Theology thus becomes an ascending spiral of contemplation. Much the same thing happens in the liturgy of Christian initiation. A given aspect of the mystery will be introduced and developed from one angle; then, at a later point, it will be picked up again and developed in new yet complementary ways, reinforcing what has gone before while at the same time encouraging fresh insights.

The difference between these two approaches can be illustrated by consideration of the place of the Holy Spirit in the baptismal process, in Christian initiation. The attentive reader may have noticed earlier that no mention was made of the place of chrismation/confirmation in the baptismal process. In the practice of the Orthodox Church, of course, anointing with chrism, accompanied by the words "Seal of the gift of the Holy Spirit," immediately follows baptism understood in the narrow sense of the word and precedes reception of the eucharist. In many Western Christian churches an anointing and/or hand-imposition (confirmation) occurs at roughly the same point. In popular presentations of baptism there is sometimes a tendency to identify this chrismation/confirmation as *the* pneumatic moment in the baptismal process. Its relationship to what has preceded it is then explained along the following lines: Aquatic baptism is to oleaginous chrismation as the Christ event is to the Spirit event, as Pascha/Easter is to Pentecost, as dying to sin is to the bestowal of new life.[7] Sometimes, in fact, baptism (in the narrow sense) comes to be associated chiefly with the negative aspect of Christian initiation. What really counts for being fully initiated is the positive aspect, chrismation/confirmation, the perfecting of baptism by reception of the Holy Spirit so that, in phrases like "of water and the Spirit," the *and* is taken as disjunctive rather than conjunctive. According to such an approach, the baptismal process is linear, one-directional. It consists of a series of stages through which the initiate passes, leaving one behind as he or she advances to the next, eventually to full membership in the eucharistic assembly which is the church. While this approach recognizes that early stages prepare one for the later stages, there is little sense that the

---

7. Among Western Christian writers see, for example, Gregory Dix, *The Theology of Confirmation in Relation to Baptism* (London: 1953).

later stages reinforce and develop what one has received earlier, that in various ways they recall and revisit the earlier stages and provide an opportunity for viewing them from a new perspective.

There are several things wrong with this approach. As those familiar with the history of liturgy will immediately note, the shape of Christian initiation in the Christian East in antiquity was originally quite different from the one presupposed by the linear approach just sketched. In the West and some parts of the East, the sequence was just as has been described — immersion in water, anointing along with hand imposition, and then reception of the eucharist. In many parts of the East, however, — Syria, Cappadocia, and even Constantinople — the sequence originally was different. Anointing *preceded* the immersion in water, and there was no post-baptismal anointing; the next major action was reception of the eucharist.[8] This sequence may be unfamiliar to us and strike us as rather odd, but it is very ancient. One can see it already in Acts, where the baptism of Paul is *preceded* by imposition of hands by Ananias (Acts 9:17-19), the baptism of Cornelius and his household is *preceded* by the descent of the Holy Spirit (Acts 10), the baptism of the three thousand (Acts 2) is *preceded* by the Pentecostal outpouring of the Spirit, and with the baptism of Queen Candace's eunuch, the entire initiative is the Spirit's (Acts 8). One can see the same sequence elsewhere in the New Testament as well — in 1 John 5:7, for example, which speaks of "the Spirit, the water, and the blood" in that order.

This sequence is not just a liturgical curiosity. Behind it lie some important theological insights. What is the relationship between Son and Spirit? On the one hand, the Son promises to send the comforter; he sends the Spirit into the world; and in the Church, by the power of the Holy Spirit, the reconciling work of the Son continues. This, the Western pattern of initiation presents very effectively. But the Holy Spirit, "who spoke by the prophets," also foreruns the Son, indwells him, fashions him even in his mother's womb, and manifests him in the Jordan precisely as the Christ, the anointed one. In this perspective there is no disjunction between Son and Spirit or subordination of one to the other. Rather, their relationship is reciprocal; they are "God's two hands," to use St. Irenaeus's homely phrase.

8. For a succinct presentation of these two "aboriginal patterns" of Christian initiation see Aidan Kavanagh, *The Shape of Baptism: The Rite of Christian Initiation* (New York: Pueblo, 1978), pp. 40-54.

This theological insight has important implications for Christian initiation. Consider what St. Gregory of Nyssa has to say about the appropriateness of the image of anointing:

> The notion of anointing suggests in a mysterious way that there is no distance between the Son and the Spirit. In effect, just as between the surface of the body and the unction of oil neither reason nor sensation knows any intermediary, so also the contact of the Son with the Spirit. And likewise, for him who would come in contact with the Son through faith, it is necessary to have experience of contact with the chrism. No member, as it were, can be left naked of the Holy Spirit. This is why confession of the Lordship of the Son is made in the Spirit by those who receive him, the Spirit in every respect forerunning those who approach in faith.[9]

The Holy Spirit "who spoke by the prophets" is also the one who enables us to understand their message, who enables us truly to hear the Word. The Holy Spirit enables us to call Jesus Lord, to make the baptismal "I believe" our own. As the passage from St. Gregory of Nyssa suggests, the Holy Spirit, as symbolized in the baptismal anointing, is, as it were, the medium in and through which we touch Christ and are refashioned to become his body, to become anointed ones, Christians, even as he is *the* anointed one, the Christ. We are baptized *into* Christ *(eis Christon)* and "put on Christ" *in* the Holy Spirit *(en to haghio pneumati)*. And at every moment, Christian initiation reveals this continuing action in and of the Holy Spirit, from initial evangelization, when the Spirit points to the Son, through the exorcisms, the blessing of the oil and water, and the blessing of the candidates themselves, to the eucharist in which Christ is made present by the power of the Holy Spirit. Eastern liturgies call attention to this in many ways, chiefly by multiplying pneumatic references which occur and recur throughout the rites of initiation: insufflations, hand-impositions, anointings of several sorts, *zeon* (hot water) added to the eucharistic cup, etcetera. One should be cautious, therefore, about identifying chrismation as *the* sacrament of the Holy Spirit as though that were the extent of the Spirit's presence and action.

A proper understanding of the place of the Holy Spirit in Christian initiation also helps us understand the meaning of baptism — in its comprehensive sense — as *sacrament* or *mysterion*. Baptism is a gracious gift of

9. *On the Holy Spirit,* PG 45:1321A-B.

God, whereby through created realities we enter into participation in divine life itself. Ultimately God is both the giver and the gift. Therefore, as Michael Root has observed, baptism "is not a 'human work,' either in the sense that it is a merely human invention or in the sense that the primary agent in baptism is either the baptizing community or the baptized individual."[10] Baptism does not depend on human qualifications and achievements. It is open to young and old, weak and strong. This is because "baptism is a work of God, both in the sense that it is divinely instituted and in the sense that the decisive agent in baptism is God, acting through the Holy Spirit within the church which baptizes."[11] Baptism in the narrow sense, chrismation, and eucharist may indeed be moments when this divine initiative is particularly conspicuous. But these three "sacraments" should not be divorced from their wider context as though God were not also at work in the Spirit throughout the process. Baptism both in its narrow sense and in its more comprehensive sense is God's gift to us. As Root puts it, "in baptism we are [all] receivers,"[12] young and old, weak and strong. "By grace" we are "saved through faith" (Eph. 2:8). In relation to baptism this means through trusting reception of what we are given, from our first response to the stirrings of the Spirit in the depths of our being, whereby we are enabled truly to hear the Word of God, to our reception of the Spirit-filled Word made flesh in the eucharistic meal. At every step of the way, we "lean into life" by leaning on God.

Let us turn to some of the implications of baptism thus understood for ecclesiology, for our understanding of the "one holy, catholic, and apostolic Church" confessed in the creed. Baptism is, first of all, the sacrament of our unity with Christ, of our participation in his paschal mystery. But to be baptized into Christ means to be baptized into his body, which is the church (1 Cor. 12:13). Baptism is initiation into the mystery of Christ and initiation into the church. It is the sacrament of our unity *with* Christ and at the same time the sacrament of our unity *in* Christ. We see a practical application of this in the sequel to Peter's preaching on Pentecost: "So those who received his word were baptized, and there were added that day about three thousand souls. And they devoted themselves to the apostles'

---

10. In a study paper entitled "Baptism and the Unity of the Church," in a volume of the same title, ed. Michael Root and Risto Saarinen (Grand Rapids: Eerdmans, 1988), p. 16. The author is deeply indebted to Prof. Root for sharing his invaluable paper and insights in advance of publication.

11. "Baptism and the Unity of the Church," pp. 16-17.

12. "Baptism and the Unity of the Church," p. 18.

teaching and fellowship, to the breaking of bread and the prayers" (Acts 2:41-42). To be baptized means to be "added" to the church, to enter into a very tangible apostolic community united in eucharist and prayer.

This recognition of the ecclesial dimension of baptism has been developed in various ways in the course of Christian history. Consider St. Cyprian, in the third century, as he addressed the problem of the schism of the Novatianists, who split with the Church Catholic over certain questions of penitential discipline. The Novatianists were outside the church, Cyprian insisted, deprived of the Holy Spirit and therefore incapable of giving the Holy Spirit in baptism. Therefore those "baptized" among them, if they should seek to enter the church, must be (re)baptized with the church's baptism, with real baptism. Cyprian's position on Novatianist baptism is fully consistent with his ecclesiology, an ecclesiology dominated by the idea of unity. "It has been handed down to us that there is one God and one Christ and one hope and one faith and one Church and one baptism appointed only in that one Church."[13] Outside that one church, not even the martyr's "baptism of public confession and blood . . . avails anything to salvation because there is no salvation outside the Church."[14] But still more can be said about Cyprian's ecclesiology. Consider how frequently he uses words like "inside" and "outside." Consider also his favorite imagery: The church is a walled garden, a sealed fountain, the ark of Noah well tarred to keep out the defiling waters of this world. Its charismatic and institutional limits coincide exactly. And as one observer has tartly remarked, "The Church which Cyprian imagines here is not the people which God has called to salvation but the institution through which he dispenses it to them."[15] In the midst of the walled garden preside the bishops, who "water the thirsting people of God by divine permission," who "guard the boundaries of the life-giving fountains."[16] For Cyprian, then, the church is above all an institution, whose unity depends not so much on a common faith and sacramental life as on the unity of the episcopate.

What can be said about Cyprian's baptismal practice and sacramental theology? Was his position that of the early church as a whole? This often is asserted by self-styled Orthodox traditionalists today. According to them, Cyprian's position, so deeply rooted in his ecclesiology, was that of

13. *Epistle* 69.12.

14. *Epistle* 73.21.

15. André d'Halleux, "Orthodoxie et catholicisme: Un seul baptême?" *Revue Théologique de Louvain* 11 (1980): 416-52 at 435.

16. *Epistle* 73.11.

the early church as a whole and should be ours today. In principle, such traditionalists would argue, all those baptized "outside the church" are unbaptized; if they seek to enter the Orthodox Church, we should rebaptize them; and if we have not done so in the past or choose not to do so now, this is simply a matter of economy — *oikonomia,* a concession to pressing pastoral considerations, and not because we recognize anything of spiritual significance in their previous baptism.[17] But in fact early church sources give only very limited support to the traditionalists' claim.

Certainly it is possible to find patristic texts that sound "Cyprianic." Many passages from early Christian writers — ranging from Tertullian on one end of the theological spectrum to Clement of Alexandria on the other — indicate widespread rejection of heretic baptism. It is important, however, to keep in mind what these writers meant by "heretic." They had in mind the gnostics, who clearly did not confess the same God and the same Christ as Christians do, who were no more Christians then than Christian Scientists are today. Such folks must indeed be baptized with the Church's baptism. But what of those who are not heretics in this radical sense of the word, who might rather be described as schismatics? What, for example, of Novatian, who — as Cyprian's opponents argued at the time — "holds the same law as the Catholic Church holds, baptizes with the same symbol with which we baptize, knows the same God the Father, the same Christ the Son, the same Holy Spirit . . ."?[18] Against such arguments, Cyprian advances a counter-argument: The Novatianists are heretics; they falsify the faith professed at baptism, because "when they say, 'Do you believe in the remission of sins and life everlasting through the Holy Church?' they lie. . . ."[19] According to Cyprian, the Novatianists are heretics every bit as much as the gnostics are, because they falsify the faith, and therefore they must be received by (re)baptism. But note how, for Cyprian, the focus of faith has shifted from the doctrine of one God, one Lord Jesus Christ, and the Holy Spirit, to the doctrine of church. The Novatianists are

17. On the subject of "economy" in modern Orthodox thought see, among others, F. J. Thomson, "Economy: An Examination of the Various Theories of Economy Held within the Orthodox Church, with Special Reference to the Economical Recognition of Non-Orthodox Sacraments," *Journal of Theological Studies* N.S. 16 (1965): 368-420; Abp. Pierre L'Huillier, "L'économie dans la tradition de l'Eglise Orthodoxe," *Kanon: Jahrbuch der Gesellschaft für das Recht der Östkirchen* 6 (1983): 19-38; and John H. Erickson, "Sacramental 'Economy' in Recent Roman Catholic Thought," *The Jurist* 48 (1988): 653-67.

18. *Epistle* 69.7

19. *Epistle* 69.7

heretics precisely because they are "outside" that universal episcopal confederation which for Cyprian is the one church.

In fact, if we examine patristic texts and early church practice more closely, we will see that a distinction is made between the forms that separation from the church can take and therefore between modes of reception. It is enough here to cite St. Basil the Great, who indicates with approval that "the ancients" distinguished between heresies, schisms, and illegal congregations: "heresies, those who are completely broken off and as regards the faith itself, alienated; schisms, those at variance with one another for certain ecclesiastical reasons and questions that admit of a remedy; illegal congregations, assemblies brought into being by insubordinate presbyters or bishops, and by uninstructed laymen."[20] As examples of heretics, St. Basil gives Montanists, Manicheans, and various gnostic groups whose understanding of God and of God's relation to creation was altogether at variance with the Christian faith and who signaled this (in the case of the Montanists) by their use of a falsified baptismal formula ("In the name of the Father and of the Son and of the Lord Montanus"). Such baptisms, Basil states, the ancients quite properly rejected. On the other hand, he notes, they accepted the baptism not only of those coming from illegal congregations but also of schismatics — and in Basil's understanding this category included many groups, such as the Novatianists, which differed with the church on some very serious doctrinal issues, but which nonetheless were "of the church." In time, of course, the term "heretic" comes to be applied to many of these groups; in part this was so that civil legislation against heretics could be enforced against them. But the practice of the church, as set forth in a whole series of liturgical and canonical texts, continued to distinguish between heretics in the earlier sense of the word, who were to be received by baptism, and those who were to be received by anointing with chrism or simply by profession of faith.[21]

We see in Christian history, then, at least two ways in which the ecclesial implications of baptism have been worked out, two positions, the Cyprianic and the "Basilian." Of these, the Cyprianic position has always had a certain appeal among the Orthodox, and it certainly has today in tra-

---

20. In *Epistle* 188.1, his first "canonical epistle," which has since been included in the basic *corpus canonum* of the Orthodox Church, canon 1.

21. For the canonical and historical dossier see John H. Erickson, "Divergencies in Pastoral Practice in the Reception of Converts," in *Orthodox Perspectives on Pastoral Praxis,* ed. Theodore Stylianopoulos (Brookline, Mass.: Holy Cross Orthodox Press, 1988), pp. 149-77.

ditionalist circles. Among other things, it satisfies a psychological need to define clearly the limits of the church. We like to be able to say who "belongs to the church" and who does not. We like to know who is a "member" and who is not. We like the assurance of being part of an elite group, of knowing that we are "inside" the one true church, "outside" of which there is no salvation. And the Cyprianic position also fits rather well with the linear approach to Christian initiation that was described earlier. It allows us to say that at this point someone is "outside" the church but at this point he is "inside." But this position fits less well with the "circular" approach to Christian initiation that one finds in Eastern liturgy and with the understanding of the Holy Spirit that underlies Eastern liturgy and theology. Here the Basilian position, while perhaps less satisfying psychologically, corresponds better to the nature of the church itself. For the church is not just an institution, *in*stituted by Christ long ago but thereafter on its own, free to do what it wishes, to make and break its own rules until Christ comes again in glory. The church also is being *con*stituted by the Holy Spirit at each new moment in history, in each new context, and therefore the church is obliged to heed the promptings of the Spirit, to discern where the Spirit is at work even now forming the body of Christ, even if this means looking outside the institutional limits of the church as we perceive them.

Earlier I said that baptism is initiation into the mystery of Christ and initiation into the church. And this clearly is but one initiation, one sacrament. But what is the relationship between the church and the mystery of Christ? Obviously much depends on what we understand by "the church" and by "the mystery of Christ," by the Christian faith itself. The problem with the Cyprianic position, in my estimation, is that it tends to forget that the church, like the person being baptized, is a "receiver." The church is a "dependent reality," with its fundamental marks or attributes — unity, holiness, catholicity, apostolicity — a gift of God. It is not self-subsistent, possessing life in itself. Rather, like the Christian, it lives by grace through faith. The church depends on Christ who shed his lifeblood for her, and on the Holy Spirit, the "giver of life." To put matters rather bluntly, by concentrating on the institutional context of baptism rather than on its faith content, the Cyprianic position tends to substitute faith in the church for faith in God — Father, Son, and Holy Spirit.

While ostensibly maintaining a "high" ecclesiology, Cyprian and his self-appointed heirs end up with an impoverished understanding of the church. Consider Cyprian's favored imagery for the church: walled garden, sealed fountain, ark of Noah. . . . These are static images, exclusive images, images suggesting no possibility of growth and development. His approach stands in contrast to the rich variety of imagery that we find in the Bible and that the fathers further develop. Here we find a wide variety of direct images — the church as temple, vine, paradise, body — and an even greater variety of types of the Church: Eve, Mary, but also Tamar, Rahab, Mary Magdalene, the Canaanite woman, Zacchaeus. . . . In other words, we find in the Bible and the fathers not just images of achieved perfection, which might incline us to hold a triumphalist and exclusive view of the church, but also images of repentance, conversion, and striving. Such images should be kept in mind when we consider baptism. In baptism, the church is built up not just in the sense that another member is added, that someone who was "outside" now is "inside." The church is built up because in the one being baptized, the church sees herself, sees her conversion, sees her own paschal faith, and thus the church is edified. The building up of the church in baptism thus is complementary: It is the building up of faith, not just in the baptizand but in each one of us.

(Here, it could be noted, the church sees herself also in the one not yet baptized, in the catechumen. Consider the rubric for the conversion of a Manichean or Jew in the ancient Byzantine *Euchologion:* "After the convert has done all this before the Church [renounced his previous errors], he has become a Christian, that is, we consider him a non-baptized Christian, as in the case of Christian infants, who ought to be baptized."[22] A non-baptized Christian! The Cyprianic position would have difficulty with such an expression; the Basilian would not.)

To understand properly the relationship between the church and the mystery of Christ, we must carefully assess what we mean by "church," but we must also consider what we mean by "the mystery of Christ." As was pointed out earlier, modern Orthodox presentations of sacramental theology often adopt the linear, analytical approach typical of the West — and in this respect they have quite a lot in common with Cyprian. What happens at early stages is perhaps not spiritually insignificant, but it is simply preparatory in nature, something that will be transcended at the moment one passes from "outside" to "inside," whether the dividing line between

---

22. Ed. Miguel Arranz, "Les sacrements de l'ancien Euchologe constantinopolitain (2)," *Orientalia Christiana Periodica* 49 (1983): 66, cited by David Petras, "The Individual and Catechesis," *Diakonia* 20 (1986): 152-74 at 164.

"outside" and "inside" is placed at baptism in the narrow sense of the word (as with Cyprian), or with chrismation (as by those who emphasize this as *the* moment in which the Spirit is bestowed), or with the eucharist (as in some versions of eucharistic ecclesiology).[23] And what happens "inside" is the experience here and now of the kingdom; we have passed beyond the "not yet" of the preparatory stages to the "already" of the messianic banquet. Popular presentations of the eucharist — at least among the Orthodox — so often speak of the eucharist as the banquet of the kingdom, the point at which history intersects with the *eschaton*, that we lose sight of its proleptic nature. We forget that the eucharist is but a foretaste of the kingdom, not its final realization. And then, this tendency towards a realized eschatology begins to creep from the eucharist into other aspects of church life, so that the church *qua* church comes to be seen as perfect in every respect. Its dependence on Christ, and him crucified, is forgotten. We want the glory and forget the cross.

The "circular" understanding of Christian initiation sketched earlier may offer an important corrective at this point. What happens in the "early stages" of Christian initiation — the catechumenate, baptism in the narrow sense, chrismation, etcetera — is not something that is then surpassed, at least not in this earthly life. The paschal content of baptism — understood in its full sense — must inform every aspect of our Christian life, including the eucharist. Aidan Kavanagh has put the matter very succinctly:

> The whole economy of *becoming* a Christian, from conversion and catechesis through the eucharist, is thus the fundamental paradigm for *remaining* a Christian. The experience of baptism in all its paschal dimension, together with the vivid memory of it in the individual and the sustained anamnesis of it in every sacramental event enacted by the community at large, constitute not only the touchstone of Catholic orthodoxy but the starting point for all catechesis, pastoral endeavor, missionary effort, and liturgical celebration in the Church. The paschal mystery of Jesus Christ dying and rising still among his faithful ones at

---

23. Consider, for example, Gennadios Limouris, "The Eucharist as the Sacrament of Sharing: An Orthodox Point of View," in *Orthodox Visions of Ecumenism*, ed. Gennadios Limouris (Geneva: WCC Publications, 1994), p. 254: "The boundaries of the body of Christ depend entirely on the eucharistic life. Outside that life, humanity is ruled by alien powers. Separation and destruction can only be averted by those who unite in Christ and prepare themselves for the joint assembly of the eucharist."

Easter in baptism is what gives the Church its radical cohesion and mission, putting it at the center of a world made new.[24]

But let us be very clear about what the paschal content of our baptismal faith is. It is focused on Jesus Christ, who was "crucified for us under Pontius Pilate, and suffered and was buried," and who "on the third day rose again according to the Scriptures." And while Jesus "rose again on the third day," we who are baptized into him still "await the resurrection of the dead." In this life, even after baptism, even in the midst of the eucharistic feast, we still hear his words, "If anyone would be my disciple, let him take up his cross daily, and follow me." The mystery of baptism, of union with Christ in his redeeming suffering and death, is a life-long reality, and so are the demands that flow from it. As the late Byzantine theologian Nicholas Cabasilas observes, "The life in Christ originates in this life and arises from it. It is perfected, however, in the life to come, when we shall have reached that last day."[25] We have not yet reached that last day.

24. *The Shape of Baptism,* pp. 160-63. Kavanagh continues: "To know Christ sacramentally only in terms of bread and wine is to know him only partially, in the dining room as host and guest. . . . Two main forces among others have traditionally balanced this tendency, and checked its spread. The first has been the attempt at keeping the notion of 'eucharist-as-meal' in tension with a notion of 'eucharist-as-sacrifice.' . . . The second force that has traditionally balanced and checked the spread of an attenuated eucharistic knowledge of Christ has been baptismal." On the relationship between the eucharist and baptism, see also D. Guenther, *Baptism as Corrective to Realized Ecclesiology* (unpublished Master of Divinity thesis, St. Vladimir's Orthodox Theological Seminary, 1994), p. 126: "The Thanksgiving offered by the Church also has as its essential content the passion of Christ. . . . the primary purpose of the Thanksgiving meal is to extend, in the experience of the baptized, the baptismal reality of Christ's passion, that is, Christ within us, in agony until time is completed, into the Light of His glorious Resurrection. Baptism is, then, . . . inasmuch as its essential content is the Passion, the paradigmatic content of the Thanksgiving."

25. *Life in Christ* 1.1, trans. C. J. de Catanzaro (Crestwood, N.Y.: St. Vladimir's Seminary Press, 1974), p. 43.

The Eucharist as the Criterion of Orthodoxy: A Study of St. Ignatius of Antioch

K. PAUL WESCHE

In many churches today, the once impregnable fortress of orthodox Christian doctrine has crumbled, not from without but from within. Doctrines and practices at one time presupposed as axiomatic have been dismissed as out of touch and irrelevant. In the name of cultural relevance, the doctrine of the Trinity no longer merits in Christian apologetic even an appendix; it is simply ignored or rejected altogether. Where it is maintained, its inner content is wholly replaced by a substance bearing a more philosophically correct character. The outer shell of the doctrine is left intact; one sees a three in one, a one in three, but beyond that the divine revelation of the Godhead is dismissed *a priori* as the product of human religious imagination, and *Father, Son,* and *Holy Spirit* are painlessly replaced by another trinitarian god whose names and personal character are more in tune with the spirit of the age.

If there is no divine revelation to speak of, then confessing and proclaiming Jesus' consubstantiality with the Father is irrelevant, and along with that his divine Sonship and his incarnation as the Second *Adam* begotten without human seed from the holy Virgin, the Second *Eve.* Nor does the continued confession of "Christ" compel one to embrace the catholic doctrine of the Trinity, since "Christ" has been removed from the pneumatological context of its natural setting in biblical Judaism, where it refers to the "bearer of God's Holy Spirit." In its new contemporary environment of religious pluralism, "Christ" is now conceived independently of Jesus since it is a designation that refers no longer to a particular divine person, but to the central principle governing one's psychology or religious outlook, whatever that might be. The result of such an exchange of terms is that anything now can pass itself off as Christian.

Once the air has been purified of all supernatural fragrance the way is clear to introduce to the now plugged olfactory tubes of religious sensibility the odor of innovative liturgical practices, which are promoted as more relevant but in reality are steps in a program serving non-Christian philosophical agendas. Having seen the Lord God of Israel off at the depot, the natives can get on with the final step of their program. Set free from the tyranny of biblical commandments and its avenging God, they need no longer concern themselves with the necessity to identify and acknowledge personal sin in the working out of their salvation. They can now enjoy a feel-good religion, worshiping a bemused god who no longer convicts, but sanctions as alternative ways of life deeds and lifestyles condemned in holy Scripture and in apostolic tradition as the way of death.

None of these heresies, of course, are strangers to the church, but there is a novelty to their contemporary existence; whereas they once paraded in full costume only outside the city walls, gaining entrance within the gates only by subterfuge, they now find themselves welcome *within* the gates in full drag and are embraced as fashionable ideas by religious leaders of confessions once known for their firm defense of trinitarian and christological orthodoxy. Anyone who dares to defend the real vitality of the ancient catholic tradition is now tagged as positively medieval — as though the provincialism worn by such a tag is self-evident — and then brushed aside without further ado; and no one shows the savvy or the nerve to hold those making the accusation accountable for their charge. These heresies are now so confused in the public perception with Christian belief, that the beliefs and practices of the ancient catholic church are dismissed with a superior air as impotent, even repugnant, gray-hairs whose flourishing belongs to a bygone era of human history. The *contemporary* Christian church — apart from the ridiculous-looking groups of hysterical fundamentalists and TV evangelists, themselves fragmented into their own parochial camps — is then identified with the bland syncretistic mishmash that has replaced the rigor and clarity of the ancient doctrines; and *its* main contribution to society is to provide a religious flavor to the secular values and political agendas of contemporary western culture.

And yet, I do not believe that the infiltration of these heretical ideas within the gates of the church is the real crisis facing Christians today. The real crisis is the theological confusion and wrangling one finds this infiltration provoking among those who would claim to be keepers of the gates. This confusion is the result of an inability to agree on what should be upheld as essential to Christian belief and praxis, and what should be relegated to the pile of *adiaphora;* and this inability to settle on what is authentically Christian exposes the real cause of the crisis facing Christians today: Do they really know the criterion by which to distinguish authentic Christian belief and praxis from what is not? Do they really know where to find that winnowing fork which alone can separate the wheat from the chaff, catholicity from sectarianism, orthodoxy from heresy? Is it that which is believed everywhere by everyone, is it an ecclesiastical *magisterium,* a theological or confessional *principle* (e.g., justification by grace through faith, or the sovereignty of God, or entire sanctification as a definite second work of grace subsequent to regeneration), is it holy *Scripture,* or is it racial, social, and sexual equality?

The confusion among Christians today is in fact the final outcome of several centuries of church history in which the keepers of the gates have unknowingly, and sometimes with good intentions, satisfied themselves with *derived* theological principles as the touchstone of orthodoxy. Different keepers have settled on different derived theological principles as the criterion of orthodoxy, and the result has been schism and fragmentation. Holding his cherished derivation close to the breast as the key to authentic Christianity, each keeper has separated from the others in a huff, and has set up his own city with his own gates and his own gatekeepers. The multiplication of confessions and denominations all claiming to be *Christian,* the distortions of the Christian faith that are generated by a derived theological principle playing as the criterion of orthodoxy, and the subsequent harm done to human souls as they try to squeeze into garments made by tailors who, within the structure of their derived theological systems, can fit the ancient catholic doctrines neither to human nature nor to the human existential condition, have brought down upon Christians a deserved scorn and contempt. The harm inflicted by religious systems claiming to be authentically catholic while grounded in derived theological principles renders the victim open to anything *but* the catholic tradition since that is associated with the cause of the pain; beliefs parading as *Christian,* but offering something distinct from *catholicity* can therefore expect to find a receptive and undiscerning audience.

In such a troubled environment as this which Christians have created

for themselves, St. Ignatius' teaching concerning the criterion of orthodoxy and the marks of catholicity may come to beleaguered lovers of the
true catholic church as a soothing salve with a fragrance all the more pungent as its sweet-smelling aroma is contrasted to the odor of many present-day understandings of the church. By saying this, of course, I register
nothing more than my own assent to St. Ignatius' teaching. This assent is
merely a response to and not the substance of the conclusions deriving
from the following historical study; the reader may therefore learn something about St. Ignatius from this study even if he chooses to leave it with a
different opinion. At the same time, however, this assent expresses a conviction that the ecclesiology articulated by this second-century *doctor
ecclesiae* is more relevant for our age, and any age, than any church reformer's could hope to be; and that only a positive and courageous assent
to the implications inherent in St. Ignatius' ecclesiology can heal Christians today of their separation and restore them to authentic catholicity;
for, it reminds us what the only true criterion of orthodoxy can be, on
which alone Christian theology and practice may be restored to its healing
and life-giving power, and heresy routed from the altar and pulpit.

What the Criterion of Orthodoxy Is Not

St. Ignatius, bishop of Antioch, lived in an age very much like our own. Society was avowedly pagan and pluralistic; the church was threatened not
only by persecution without, but by syncretism and division within. This
pluralistic syncretism, threatening the church at a time when the first generation succeeding the apostles was striving to preserve faithfully the identity of the apostolic church against new challenges, gave to the bishops'
task of rightly defining the faith a particularly critical urgency. Around the
year 110 A.D., St. Ignatius took time to exhort by letter the leading
churches in the regions through which he was passing on his way to mar-
tyrdom in Rome. In these letters we find a clear and I would say widely forgotten ecclesiology, certainly in terms of identifying the criterion of catholic orthodoxy.[1]

1. The text on which the present study is based is that established by J. B. Lightfoot
and J. R. Harmer in *The Apostolic Fathers: Greek Texts and English Translations of Their Writings,* 2nd edition, revised and edited by Michael W. Holmes (Grand Rapids: Baker Book
House, 1992).

The traditional understanding of St. Ignatius emphasizes the central place of the bishop in his ecclesiology. There is no question that the bishop occupies a fundamental place in St. Ignatius' church; the fact that eucharistic worship is valid (or sure and trustworthy — βεβαιοτης) only when under the authority of the bishop makes clear the bishop's indispensable role in the church.[2] Indeed, St. Ignatius will go so far as to say that any group which is out of communion with (χωρις) the bishop, the presbyters, and the deacons cannot be called church.[3] From the many assertions of this kind there can be no doubt that for St. Ignatius, the structure of the church, or the form in which the church's existence is concretized, is episcopal and hierarchical, so that if there is no bishop, there is no church. In whatever place the church comes into existence, the form it will naturally and necessarily take is episcopal and hierarchical. (There is much more to this seemingly mundane ecclesiological fact than meets the eye; its implications give to the church's missionary character and to Christian spirituality and belief an ecclesial concreteness that reveals the church's episcopal structure to be a manifestation of the church's character as the extension of Jesus' incarnation; but we dare not enter into an excursus on this since it would take us far beyond the spatial limits set for this study.)

Nevertheless, as constitutive as the bishop might be of the church's existential structure, and as often as St. Ignatius stresses unity with the bishop as a guarantee of orthodoxy, a careful study of his letters suggests quite clearly, or so it seems to me, that the episcopal structure of the church is not *the* touchstone of catholic orthodoxy. One cannot say without qualification that the bishop *constitutes* the church, for even the bishop is made a bishop by something else in the church. Settling no further than upon the episcopal structure of the church as constitutive of the church produces an identification of catholicity with magisterial power and authority, leading to an authoritarian clericalism that excludes the laity from the responsible administration of the church's faith. Indeed, if one's view of the church stops at its episcopal structure, the vital unity between episcopacy and the church's missionary activity, spirituality, and incarnate character cannot be seen or really understood.

That St. Ignatius does not understand the episcopal structure in itself to be *the* criterion of orthodoxy is suggested for one thing by his frequent admonitions to adhere to the true teaching of the church, which he repeats

---

2. *To the Smyrneans* 8.1.
3. *To the Trallians* 3.1.

as often as he exhorts the faithful to adhere firmly to the bishop. "I want you to be firmly convinced about the birth and the suffering and the resurrection [of Jesus Christ our God] which took place during the time of the governorship of Pontius Pilate. These things were truly and most assuredly done by Jesus Christ, our hope, *and from this hope may none of you ever be turned aside.*"[4] This is *the* teaching of the church for St. Ignatius, and it is the possession of and adherence to this teaching that constitutes one of the marks identifying the catholic church from the heretics. The fervor and frequency of St. Ignatius' warnings to flee from the "wicked teaching of the ruler of this age," his disgust for the stench of those who do not acknowledge the flesh and blood of Christ our God,[5] calling them "corpse-bearers (νεκροφορος)" and "advocates of death,"[6] his fervent admonitions to adhere to the true teaching of Jesus Christ indicate rather clearly that the bishop stands as the guarantee of orthodoxy because he possesses the true teaching of the church concerning Jesus the Christ.

St. Ignatius had not the experience of sixteenth- or twenty-first-century Christians, behind whom extends a long field of painful church history heavily littered with vacillating, apostate, and heretical bishops. In St. Ignatius' time, this teaching was firmly held by all the bishops he knew, and so to include the bishops in his condemnation of those who might teach otherwise does not occur to him. But his list of those who are condemned if they teach otherwise is all-inclusive, and so it would by extension fall even upon the bishops: "Let *no one* be misled," he says. "Even the heavenly beings and the glory of angels and the rulers, both visible and invisible, are also subject to judgment, if they do not believe in the blood of Christ."[7] The bishops are for St. Ignatius, then, a guarantee of orthodoxy because of their *teaching* concerning Jesus Christ, not simply because they are bishops.

Does this mean then that the true teaching of the incarnate God, Jesus Christ, is the real criterion of orthodoxy? No. Certainly it is *an* indispensable and non-negotiable criterion of orthodoxy, just as is unity with the bishop, but the fineness of analysis to which I am subjecting the thought of St. Ignatius and the depths I am trying to fathom in his understanding of the church prevent identifying even this as *the* criterion of

4. *To the Magnesians* 11.1.

5. Δυσωδιαν, which he contrasts to the sweet-smelling myrrh of incorruptibility breathed on the church by the incarnate Jesus: *To the Ephesians* 17.1.

6. *To the Smyrneans* 5.1 & 2.

7. *Smyrneans* 6.1.

catholic orthodoxy; for, even this points beyond itself to something deeper in the church out of which the episcopate and its teaching emerge. The fact that the criterion of orthodoxy cannot be reduced to a teaching or to an episcopal structure has radical consequences for the understanding of *catholicity* and of *church*, and everything else associated with the church. It distinguishes a truly catholic ecclesiology from a heretical ecclesiology.

What the Criterion of Orthodoxy Is

The criterion of catholic orthodoxy for St. Ignatius is the *eucharist:* not just the fact that there is something called a eucharist, or even that the eucharist is rightly administered — for the heretics had their sacraments and eucharist, too, which they may even have administered very nicely — but that eucharist alone which in reality is the living flesh and blood of Jesus Christ. There is here a densely packed nuance hidden beneath a subtly woven veil. When that nuance is exposed, an explosion of ecclesiological consequences far more radical than any reformer could bring about is released, that upsets many notions held of the church today. To catch the full force of St. Ignatius' *eucharistic ecclesiology,* then, let us be sure that the veil is fully lifted.

St. Ignatius lived in the atmosphere of Jewish Christianity, which means that the governing core of his theological understanding was given him by the traditions of biblical Judaism. Old Testament anthropology sees man as a creature utterly dependent on resources outside of himself for his continued existence. Man is not an indestructible particle of divine spiritual being, but a perishable, corporeal creature constituted from the dust of the ground, whose life lies in his blood. And yet, though man is a perishable creature, he yearns with his whole being for God himself. This implies that man, although a mortal creature by nature, is created with the capacity to receive the life of God, which in turn implies that man can live eternally if he is in God.[8] But man's corporeal character requires that his spiritual life in God be received in a corporeal way. Simple knowledge or intellectual assent to a spiritual teaching is not sufficient to save man from the real death he suffers; for man is not an intellect looking for escape from

---

8. This is a very densely abbreviated synopsis of the Old Testament vision of man as described in Hans Walther Wolff's study, *Anthropology of the Old Testament* (Philadelphia: Fortress Press, 1975).

the body by means of knowledge. He is a corporeal and mortal creature who perishes if he is separated from God on whom he is wholly dependent for the eternal life for which he yearns. Understanding the principles of biblical anthropology that make up the background of St. Ignatius' Christianity renders one particularly alert to the eucharistic overtones of such phrases as, "you have taken on new life in the blood of God"[9] or the "fruit of Christ's passion and resurrection by which we are made to exist."[10] Against this backdrop of Jewish anthropology, the meaning of such remarks as these is shown to be that man is made to exist and to live truly only in the life-giving blood of Jesus Christ because Jesus Christ is God.[11] The life-giving blood of Christ is the eucharist of the church, the fruit of Christ's passion and resurrection. Thus, when St. Ignatius writes: "Wherever Jesus Christ is, there is the *catholic church*,"[12] he is not thinking conceptually or intellectively as a Greek might think, but concretely as a Jew would think. That is to say, wherever Jesus Christ is concretely, tangibly, and physically present in his mystical[13] body and blood which is the eucharist, the fruit of his passion and resurrection, there is the catholic church.

The nuance of understanding that is derived from reading these and many other similar passages against the background of biblical anthropol-

9. *To the Ephesians* 1.1.

10. *To the Smyrneans* 1.2. "From the fruit of Christ's divinely blessed passion we are made to exist (αφ' ου καρπου ημεις απο του θεομακαριστου αυτου παθους)."

11. For the reader requiring documentation of every key assertion such as this, the text in *Smyrn* 1.1 may stand as the exemplar of the many passages asserting the full divinity of Christ: "I glorify Jesus Christ, the God who makes you wise."

12. *Smyrneans* 8.2. In this passage, by the way, St. Ignatius introduces into Christian literature for the first time the term "catholic church."

13. Mystical is *my* term, it is not St. Ignatius'. I insert it in various places throughout the study in an effort to keep the modern reader from seasoning the wholly Jewish flavor of St. Ignatius' sacramental theology of real presence so heavily with the Aristotelian terms of scholastic theology that it seems to taste like Greek *spanikopita*. In Eastern Orthodox theology, the bread and wine remain bread and wine, but they become in truth, in the celebration of the divine liturgy, even as they remain bread and wine, the living body and blood of Christ. Beyond this, Orthodox theology does not go in for explaining the transformation of the gifts, except to say that the body and blood of the eucharist is the *deified* humanity of the divine *Logos* who is Jesus Christ, which means that the transformation of the gifts into the body and blood of Christ takes place in a divine manner that transcends the categories of our fallen world of time and space, and therefore cannot be comprehended or explained within the philosophical terms of this world. In *this* sense do I intend the term *mystical* as a faithful hermeneutical device to signify the substance of St. Ignatius' eucharistic theology.

ogy is the key for unlocking the full force of St. Ignatius' emphasis on the church's eucharist as that which makes the church catholic. If we are to conceive of holy eucharist as St. Ignatius did, we cannot take the term to refer simply to bread and wine over which words of institution are said, or that are even covered by an *epiklesis*. He refers specifically to that particular bread and wine which are indeed the actual life-giving body and blood of Jesus Christ. That is to say, just because a community celebrates something they call *eucharist*, and just because someone says their bread and wine are the body and blood of Christ, even if it is a pope or a bishop saying so, does not make one's bread and wine actually to be so, or that community to be catholic or church in the truly Christian sense. What makes a community truly catholic and truly church is that particular eucharist alone which is in fact the actual life-giving body and blood of Jesus Christ; and that eucharist is the actual life-giving body and blood of Christ which alone is rooted in Christ's passion and resurrection.

What the Criterion of Orthodoxy Means

This nuance — that the criterion of orthodoxy is not *any* eucharist, but that eucharist *alone* which is the life-giving body and blood of Jesus Christ — cannot be stressed enough; it is the detonator in St. Ignatius' *eucharistic ecclesiology* that sets off a series of devastating explosions. By establishing as the criterion of catholic orthodoxy that particular eucharist alone which is in fact the life-giving body and blood of Jesus Christ, St. Ignatius removes the determination of orthodoxy wholly and completely from the sphere of any theological discourse or human striving or religious experience. It matters not a whit what men may say or think or believe, no matter how erudite or sophisticated; they cannot make the church or catholicity because they cannot make their eucharist to be Jesus Christ's life-giving body and blood by anything they say or do *or believe*. Is the reader offended by this? It doesn't matter; for St. Ignatius, however vigorously we may protest, our protestations and arguments cannot make our respective eucharists to be *the* eucharist of the church. The theological wranglings produced by wounded egos and offended sensibilities simply have no bearing on the fact that there is but one true eucharist: that eucharist which is in fact the living body and blood of Jesus Christ.

If the criterion of catholic orthodoxy is that eucharist which is in fact the body and blood of Jesus Christ, then the criterion of catholic orthodoxy is none other than Jesus Christ himself who is really, personally, physically, as well as spiritually and mystically present in the church in her eucharist. If this is *the* criterion of catholicity, then orthodoxy is not determined by a theological principle, or by that which is everywhere believed by everyone, or by an episcopal magisterium, or by a dogmatic proposition, or by any conciliar definition. All of these are derived and point beyond themselves to that which alone determines authentic orthodoxy: Jesus Christ himself who is really present in the church in holy eucharist which is his life-giving body and blood.

We are only beginning to tell the full impact of St. Ignatius' eucharistic ecclesiology. In this eucharistic setting, the traditional description of the church as Christ's body and blood can no longer be taken as a mystical metaphor to describe some spiritualized fellowship between the soul and some divine force that takes up its abode in one's heart in some mystical way. The description means precisely what it says. The church's mystical nature has a disturbingly corporeal character to it: the church is the body and blood of Christ in a concrete, physical way because her eucharist *is* the mystical body and blood of Christ not in a nostalgic or significatory or symbolical way, but tangibly and concretely.

But this realization immediately unleashes another explosion. If the church is the body and blood of Christ, then *we are not the church,* for we are not Christ, and we cannot make our consecrated bread and wine to be his life-giving body and blood. The very term early Christians chose to identify themselves, the *ekklesia* or "the elect" which we translate as "church," teaches as much. The term presupposes the eschatological content of its Jewish apocalyptic milieu. In the vision of Jewish apocalyptic there is only one Elect One, only one who is predestined before the ages: the Messiah or Righteous One who is to be sent by God at the end of history to vindicate the righteous. For Christians, that Elect One, the *ekklesia,* is Jesus Christ the Son of God. Therefore, individuals are not predestined before the ages to election; that is to say, individuals are not the *ekklesia,* the church. Only Christ, the Son of God is. St. Ignatius alludes to this eschatology of *ecclesial predestination* in his greeting to the Ephesians when he addresses himself not to predestined individuals, but to "the church *(ekklesia)* [i.e., to the body of Christ] which is predestined before the ages." Believers *become ekklesia,* they *become* the elect only as they *become* one body with Jesus Christ, the *ekklesia,* through the partaking of that eucharist which is in fact his life-giving body and blood.

In the wake of this explosion which obliterates any tendency to think that *we are the church,* the concomitant tendency to think that we own the church and can make the church *whatever we are* is also completely destroyed. Every notion that identifies the church with anything human except the deified humanity of Christ's life-giving body and blood is wiped out. The church is not made to exist by an episcopal hierarchy, nor does she come into realization by the coming together of believers bonded by a common belief, or a common ideology, or a common interpretation of Scripture, or a common political agenda, or a common religious experience. The church is the fruit of Christ's passion and resurrection; and that fruit is the life-giving, mystical body and blood of Christ, which is the church's eucharist. The criterion of orthodoxy therefore is not subject to the whims or erudition of human religious imagination; it cannot be exchanged for a political agenda, or altered to fit a philosophical program. One cannot judge the church and make her whatever one would like her to be; one submits to the judgment of the church. One enters and becomes catholic *ekklesia* on the church's terms, that is to say on the terms of the Elect One whose body is the church, or one does not find the church at all; for the church is not something human we make, she is something divine we *seek.*

But wait: there is no room to settle oneself, for this explosion immediately introduces another. If the church is the life-giving body and blood of Christ, the eucharist, then the church cannot be defined as a community of preachers or teachers of a gospel message telling about God's mighty deeds — "God's story" (a phrase that reveals the truly remarkable ability of modern-day theologians to transform the glory of the gospel, through the combination of two perfectly good words, into utterly insipid and meaningless drivel). In the eucharistic ecclesiology of St. Ignatius, gospel refers not to a proclamation, but to the eucharist as the mystical body and blood of Jesus Christ. The tendency to perceive the gospel primarily as a message or a teaching which is taught, to which one gives his "Amen" and which, by accepting and understanding, brings one into the gates of the kingdom, has been with the church from very early on. Such a tendency naturally finds its central point of emphasis in the Scriptures as the record of this teaching and therefore accepts as truly Christian only that which can be supported by explicit documentation from the Bible. In St. Ignatius' day this tendency was represented by *Judaizers,* heretics who believed that Jesus was fully flesh and blood, but not God. They were marked by their fundamentalist protestations: "If I do not find it in the Scriptures [αρχεια, i.e., the archives which were the Old Testament], I will not believe it in the gospel." When St. Ignatius answered, "But it is written," they retorted, "That is debatable," to which St. Ignatius replied: "For me, the Scriptures (αρχεια) are Jesus Christ; the holy Scriptures (τα αθικτα αρχεια = incorruptible or pure archives) are his cross and death, his resurrection and the faith which comes through him."[14] This final rejoinder discloses the concrete character which the gospel has for St. Ignatius. The gospel is not a story or narrative *about* Jesus Christ to which one subscribes, becoming thereby a saved believer: it is Jesus Christ himself, the partaking of whose life-giving body and blood saves the believer; for only in the eucharist does perishable, mortal man receive that mystical life-giving blood of Christ God which he needs to live eternally in the life of God. St. Ignatius says in one place: "I have taken refuge in the gospel as the flesh of Jesus."[15] No metaphor is intended here, for he goes on to explain: "The gospel possesses something distinctive, namely, the *coming* of the Savior, our Lord Jesus Christ, his suffering, and the resurrection. The *gospel is the imperishable finished work.*"[16] And in another letter, he writes: "Pay attention to the gospel in which the passion has been made clear to us and the *resurrection has been accomplished.*"[17] Now, a gospel strictly conceived as proclamation or as the narrative of God's story cannot be described as itself possessing the *coming* of the Savior, or as the *imperishable finished work,* or as that in which the resurrection *has been accomplished.* Gospel conceived strictly as proclamation or narrative points to and speaks about coming and accomplishment and *imperishable finished work;* but it is not itself the actuality of these.

One must recall that for the early church, the tradition handed on from the Lord through the apostles was not a gospel strictly conceived as proclamation, to which believers continually gave their "Amen," but rather the eucharist (1 Cor. 11:23ff.). One must recall further that the eucharist, as the consecration of the gifts, stands at the center of a liturgical cycle of daily and weekly services and offices constituted of Old and New Testament readings, prayers, hymns, and pastoral homilies. These are all borne in a liturgical movement to the celebration of the eucharist, when the hope contained in the ascetic discipline of the liturgical cycle is consummated by coming to the Messianic banquet of the church's eucharist and receiv-

---

14. *To the Philadelphians* 8.2.
15. *Philadelphians* 5.1.
16. *Philadelphians* 9.2.
17. *To the Smyrneans* 7.2.

ing the life-giving body and blood of Christ. Gospel in this eucharistic at-mosphere, even if restricted to the proclamation of the salvation won by Jesus Christ, is still experienced as but one element in the entire move-ment of the liturgical cycle that culminates in the actual entrance into Christ's passion and resurrection, which is the very substance of the gos-pel, through the partaking of his body and blood. That is to say that in the setting of the eucharist, even if gospel meant nothing more than procla-mation, the identity of the church could never be reduced to a community of proclaimers, for, in the liturgical cycle of the eucharist, church is experi-enced as the actual accomplishment of salvation. Only from within the context of this eucharistic ecclesiology is one saved from the innocuous expedient of resorting to metaphor in an effort to make any real sense of St. Ignatius' description of the gospel as that which "possesses the coming of the Savior," or as the "imperishable finished work," or as the "accom-plishment of Christ's resurrection." This divine life that one receives in the church's eucharist is what makes the church's gospel such *glad tidings*. The church's gospel does not merely *proclaim* that death has been conquered and that there is now new life in Christ, but it actually brings the believer into the *accomplishment* of that salvation through the sacramental en-trance of baptism, chrismation, and eucharist into the very passion and resurrection of Christ our God. There simply is no room here for identify-ing the church with a community of believers holding a gospel narrative rightly proclaimed, conceived as the story of God's mighty deeds. The church is that community where the Word is not simply proclaimed, but is actually *present* in that holy eucharist which is truly his body and blood; consequently the church as community is that community which has been *made* the church by becoming one body with Christ through the partaking of his actual life-giving flesh and blood in the church's eucharist.

This makes for St. Ignatius an easy test in locating the true church of Christ. The heretics refuse to acknowledge that the eucharist is the flesh of our Savior, Jesus Christ.[18] They would feel no anxiety then in separating themselves from the church, since the church for them would be nothing more than a particular teaching about God and Jesus which they don't be-lieve. Since they deny that Jesus is the Christ, the Son of God who was

---

18. *Smyrneans* 6.2. "Note well those who hold heretical opinions about the grace of Jesus Christ which came to us; note how contrary they are to the mind of God. . . . They ab-stain from the eucharist and prayer, because they refuse to acknowledge that the eucharist is the flesh of our Savior Jesus Christ, which suffered for our sins, and which the Father by his goodness raised up."

clothed in the flesh (σαρκοφορος), who truly suffered and died, *no* eucharist can be the living flesh and blood of Christ, for Christ did not exist as such.[19] Nor do they need any "blood of God" to be saved from death for they assume their souls to be by nature immortal, indestructible particles of divine being, lacking only the knowledge of their divine nature and destiny to enable them to ascend to their heavenly home above the cosmos. The church's gospel is inferior to theirs because the church's gospel has to do with a dying, fleshly God, while theirs is spiritual; it teaches a spiritual, disincarnate Christ, who only appeared to be clothed in the flesh, to suffer and to die. Their gospel is the spiritual *teaching* given by Christ, the acceptance and knowledge of which saves them by making them *gnostics,* possessors of secret divine knowledge. Salvation for them consists strictly of knowledge, *gnosis;* and there is no need for a sacrament which is in fact the flesh and blood of Jesus Christ, imparting the eternal, divine life of God. Faith conceived as an intellective act of understanding and acceptance is quite sufficient. Let the sacraments, if they are held at all, be nothing more than signs or emblems imaging in a sensible way the real thing up there in the spiritual realms, but having no power or significance in and of themselves.

For St. Ignatius the spiritual gospel of these false teachers, which denies the flesh of Christ, is proof that just as their Christ only appeared to be in the flesh and to suffer, so also they exist in appearance only.[20] In their denial that the bread and cup are the flesh and blood of God and that the Lord was σαρκοφορος and in their concomitant refusal to partake of the life-giving flesh of God they remain dead;[21] they are νεκροφοροι, bearers of a corpse,[22] carrying with them the stench of death, smug in the false hope that they will become "disembodied and spiritual (σαωματοις και δαεμονικοις)."[23] They will indeed become disembodied and spiritual, but apart from the life-giving blood of God, and this for them will be the accomplishment of their death, not of their salvation; for, men by nature are not lost particles of divine being, but perishable flesh and blood, who, apart from the life that only God can give, perish into the dust whence they were taken.

19. *Smyrneans* 5.2.

20. *Smyrneans* 2.1.

21. *Smyrneans* 7.1: "Therefore, those who deny the good gift of God perish in their contentiousness." Cf. *Smyrneans* 5.1: "[These heretics] are advocates of death rather than the truth."

22. *Smyrneans* 5.2.

23. *Smyrneans* 2.1.

At this point, one should look around. One will discover that in the last explosion, which obliterated every notion that reduces the church to a proclamatory community possessing a gospel narrative, the tendency to hold on to holy Scripture as *the* criterion of orthodoxy was also destroyed. For Scripture in the mind of St. Ignatius is not a set of books or a story but Jesus Christ himself, received in the church's eucharist. The Bible is the written record containing a faithful and true record of the prophetic expectation and the actual accomplishment of our salvation by Jesus Christ, the Son of God. Scripture too, then, points beyond itself to Jesus Christ as *the* criterion of orthodoxy. But there is no time to assimilate fully the consequences of this understanding of Scripture before another explosion even more shattering is set off that reveals once and for all the thorough radicalism of St. Ignatius' eucharistic ecclesiology. If the gospel cannot be reduced to a narrative of God's mighty deeds so that salvation cannot consist of an intellectual assent to the truth of what one has heard, then salvation cannot be had even by faith. If salvation consists not in hearing and understanding, but in being raised from death into newness of life then faith in itself is not that which *accomplishes* salvation, for faith is simply the desire of the human heart to *receive* salvation, it is the trust of the helpless creature in the power and goodness of God to accomplish that which man wants and needs to keep him from the darkness and despair of death: eternal life in intimate, loving communion with God. The eucharist of the catholic church, as the actual accomplishment of our salvation, as Christ's passion and resurrection, as the true living body and blood of Christ, as the crucified and risen Jesus Christ himself, is the consummation of faith's love; it is the mystical union for which faith longs; it is the beloved God himself whose infinite love for man created within man's bosom at the very genesis of his creation the unrelenting movement of faith's yearning whose love could be satisfied only in full union with God, a union of flesh and blood as well as of spirit. This eucharist, this accomplishment of God's loving dispensation is the grace to come, the gospel of salvation the prophets diligently searched for, seeking to know what person or time the spirit of Christ within them was indicated as he predicted the suffering of Christ and the glories to follow (1 Peter 1:10-11).

In the eucharistic ecclesiology of St. Ignatius, faith and love are far more than attitudes or dispositions of the heart. In the eucharist of the church, faith and love are incarnate as the concrete manifestations of the church's divine life received in the eucharist. St. Ignatius exhorts the faithful in the church of Tralles: "Arm yourselves with gentleness and regain your strength in *faith which is the flesh of the Lord, and in love which is the blood of Christ.*"[24] Other passages suggest that this identification of faith and love with the flesh and blood of Christ is more than metaphor as was true in his identification of gospel with the flesh of Jesus. In a passage assuming the setting of the church's eucharist, wherein he exposes the heretics by pointing out their rejection of the eucharist as the actual flesh and blood of Jesus Christ, he reminds his readers that "faith and love are *everything, nothing is preferable to them.*"[25] In another eucharistic passage, he writes: "Do not attempt to convince yourselves that anything done apart from the others is right, but, gathering together, let there be one prayer, one petition, one mind, one hope, with *love* and blameless joy, *which is Jesus Christ, than whom nothing is better.*"[26] Faith and love again are set within the context of the eucharist when he writes: "Make every effort to come together in the eucharist and glory of God (συνερχεσθαι εις ευχαριστιαν θεου και δοξαν). . . . Faith and love are the beginning and end of life; faith is the beginning, and love is the end; and *the two* when they exist in unity *are God.*"[27] Only by conceding the eucharistic content of the terms in question from their eucharistic settings can one then unlock their full meaning for St. Ignatius: nothing is preferable to faith and love because they are the flesh and blood of Christ than whom nothing is better. Faith and love are the beginning and end of life because in their union, that is to say, in the incarnation of Jesus Christ by which he unites himself to humanity, they are the flesh and blood of Jesus Christ who is God.

Only the eucharistic ecclesiology articulated by this second century *doctor ecclesiae* reveals the concrete, corporeal character of the church's divine life. This brings us immediately upon the marks of catholicity, at least as they were understood in the ecclesiology of St. Ignatius, and answers the sharp questions raised by such an understanding of the criterion of catholic orthodoxy: where then does one find that eucharist which is truly the body and blood of Christ? And how will one know that that eucharist is in fact the body and blood of Christ?

24. *To the Trallians* 8.1.
25. *To the Smyrneans* 6.1.
26. *To the Magnesians* 7.1.
27. *To the Ephesians* 13.1–14.1.

The Marks of Catholicity

The identification of faith and love with the flesh and blood of Jesus Christ reveals the character of the divine life received in the church's eucharist and identifies the marks of catholicity. The fundamental character of all the marks of catholicity is the divine, life-giving love of Jesus Christ the Son of God, for this love is the blood of God which the faithful receive in the church's eucharist and which makes them to live in the newness of Christ's divine life.

A fundamental mark of catholicity in St. Ignatius' eucharistic ecclesiology is the substantial character of the church's love. "I want the bread of God which is the flesh of Christ," St. Ignatius writes in one place, "and for drink I want his blood which is incorruptible love."[28] The flesh and blood of God, of course, are the life of God. Identifying Christ's flesh and blood with faith and love implies that the substance of divine life is divine love. That God's love should be incarnate in the blood of his humanity reveals that God's love is not an abstraction or an impersonal spiritual force; it is substantive and can be made corporeal and given to man, who must exist in a corporeal way if he is to exist, so that man can be made in his corporeal existence to live the divine life of God. God's love is hypostatized in the flesh and blood of his deified humanity and given to the faithful in the holy eucharist of the church. It mingles with their perishable human blood; it becomes the nourishment that makes up their nerves, their tissues, their bones, their flesh; it mingles with the breath they breathe until they are infused throughout the whole of their being with the flesh and blood, that is to say, with the love of God; they are made χριστοφοροι and θεοφοροι, bearers of Christ and of God.[29] Their bodies become, not in theory, but in actuality ναοφοροι and αγιαφοροι: holy, living temples that bear the Holy One.[30] For St. Ignatius' eucharistic ecclesiology, the critical point is the substantive reality of Jesus Christ's incarnation, for the reality of the church's eucharist depends upon it.[31] Because Jesus was truly made flesh, and truly suffered, and truly rose from the dead, the church's eucharist is substantively the life-giving flesh and blood of Christ; but since the substance of Christ's flesh and blood re-

---

28. Cf. *To the Romans* 7.3.

29. From this it should be clear that the Eastern Orthodox doctrine of *theosis* is inspired from within the ethos of this eucharistic ecclesiology of St. Ignatius and can only be misrepresented or imperfectly grasped apart from it.

30. *To the Ephesians* 9.2.

31. Cf. *To the Smyrneans* 1.1–2.2.

ceived in the church's eucharist is faith and love, this means that the faith and love of the church are likewise substantive. For St. Ignatius, this substantive character of the church's love, which is the very substance of the divine life received in the church's eucharist, manifests itself in substantive deeds: "Note well those who hold heretical opinions about the grace of Jesus Christ," St. Ignatius warns his readers. "They have no concern for love, none for the widow, none for the orphan, none for the oppressed, none for the prisoner or the one released, none for the hungry or thirsty."[32] The love of the church bears in its essence no resemblance to the imitations that might be produced by the heretics, for it is not rooted in a spiritual, disincarnate Christ, but in a Christ who was truly flesh and blood, who truly suffered, died, and was buried, and whose love is really and substantively received in the flesh and blood of the church's eucharist.

Together with the substantive character of the church's love is a second fundamental mark of catholicity. Since this substantive love of the church is the blood *of God* who was truly flesh and blood, who truly died, and was truly raised from the dead and ascended in glory, it carries in itself the power and sweet fragrance of Christ's resurrected, regenerating life. In the "blood of God" the faithful have taken on "newness of life."[33] The bread that they break in their gathering — the eucharist — is "the medicine of immortality, the antidote we take in order not to die but to live forever in Jesus Christ."[34] There is a sweet fragrance to this divine life of the church; it is the myrrh of incorruptibility which the Lord Jesus Christ has breathed upon the church — an obvious allusion to John's Gospel when the resurrected Lord Jesus breathed upon his disciples his divine Holy Spirit.[35] This myrrh of incorruptibility is contrasted to the stench that characterizes the teaching of the ruler of this age. That teaching carries the odor of death, for it bears witness to a phantom Christ who has no power of life since it only appears to exist. Those who give themselves to this nonexistent Christ are therefore "corpse-bearers" for they unite themselves not to a living Christ but to an apparent Christ who can give to its devotees an existence no better than its own apparent existence.[36] For St. Ignatius, only

---

32. Cf. *Smyrneans* 6.2. One might add to this list: "they have no concern for the unborn, for the weak and infirm, the aged." Selective practice of love does not qualify as *divine* love.

33. *Ephesians* 1.1.

34. *Ephesians* 20.2.

35. *Ephesians* 17.1.

36. *To the Smyrneans* 2.1 & 5.2.

those who have received Christ in the church's eucharist, who was God clothed in our flesh,[37] who was "God in man, true life in death,"[38] may taste on the tongue the body of Christ, the fountain of immortality,[39] and experience the living peace, hope, and blameless joy — which are also substantive qualities that characterize the life-giving flesh and blood of God — as divine realities in the depths of one's being in the partaking of the church's holy eucharist.[40] Accordingly, St. Ignatius exhorts the faithful "to do everything knowing that Christ dwells in us, that we may be his temples, and he may be in us as our God."[41] In the eucharistic context of the whole of St. Ignatius' thought, this exhortation can easily be rendered to mean that the love which the catholic church practices in a substantive, concrete way will be marked by a truly spiritual quality, for it is infused with the invigorating freshness of Christ's life-giving blood through the partaking of his deified humanity in the church's eucharist. Consequently, even when the faithful do things "in the flesh" their deeds have about them a divine, life-giving fragrance that distinguishes truly *catholic* love from the empty, corruptible love of the heretics, for they are done in Jesus Christ, that is to say in his spiritual, divine, life-giving flesh and blood which is the church's eucharist.[42]

Just as there is but one God, so there is but one divine life, and one divine love. The mark of love, inasmuch as it is the character of the one Lord whose living flesh and blood is received in the church's eucharist, therefore presupposes the fundamental mark of unity. This is where the

37. *Smyrneans* 5.2.

38. *Ephesians* 7.2.

39. These words form the text of the hymn sung at holy communion in the ancient liturgies of the Eastern Orthodox church, which actually reveals the thoroughly Jewish character of the church's eucharist and expresses well the mind of St. Ignatius. In the Old Testament, the term normally translated as *soul, nephesh,* actually refers to the *throat.* The throat is the organ by which needy man satisfies his thirst and hunger for food that he needs to live, and from that is extended to designate human desire for the infinite life of God: "As the hart pants for the stream, so my throat *(nephesh)* thirsts for Thee, O God!" (Ps. 42:1; cf. Wolff, *Anthropology of the Old Testament,* ch. 1, "Needy Man.") That Old Testament longing actually to drink in the life of God is consummated in the church's eucharist where the faithful drink the "mystical blood of God," and taste on their tongue how good the Lord is, whose blood is the "medicine of immortality, the antidote to death," so that they might live forever in Jesus Christ; cf. St. Ignatius, *To the Ephesians* 20.2.

40. Cf. *Magnesians* 7.1.

41. *Ephesians* 15.3.

42. *Ephesians* 8.2. "Even those things which you do carnally are spiritual, for you do all things in Jesus Christ."

episcopate and the church's teaching find their significance as criteria of orthodoxy: by his teaching, the bishop *manifests* — he does not constitute — the unity of the church. The unity of the church is constituted in the one eucharist of the church precisely because it is not a symbol, but is in fact the life-giving body and blood of Jesus Christ. Rooted in the one eucharist of the church, the bishops are united in their teaching; for the eucharist is Jesus Christ, and Jesus Christ is the mind (the γνώμη) of the Father.[43] This means that in the eucharist the bishop (together with all the faithful) receives not only the love of God, but also the mind, or the knowledge of God, for in receiving Jesus Christ, the mind of the Father, one receives the God who makes us wise.[44] The eucharistic foundation of the church is what allows St. Ignatius to say that the bishop is the mind of Jesus Christ, just as Christ is the mind of the Father,[45] for the bishop has received the mind of God in the eucharist. Accordingly, the teaching of the bishops will agree in all particulars, for their teaching is derived from the one knowledge received in the holy eucharist which is the one Lord Jesus Christ; the unity of their teaching is therefore a fundamental mark of *their* catholicity, so that adherence to the *catholic* bishops is the fundamental mark of the catholicity of the faithful.[46]

This means that catholic dogma is not subject to the whims of human theological fancy; it is not a piece of theological guesswork, or of philosophical speculation, but the articulation of the knowledge of God

43. *Ephesians* 3.2.

44. *Smyrneans* 1.1 and *Ephesians* 17.2. "Why do we not all become wise by receiving God's knowledge, which is Jesus Christ?"

45. *Ephesians* 3.2.

46. When St. Irenaeus, later in the second century, lists apostolic succession as a criterion of orthodoxy, he is saying nothing new, for apostolic succession as a mark of catholicity is inherent in the eucharistic ecclesiology of St. Ignatius. Through partaking of the one eucharist which is in fact the living body and blood of Christ, the bishops are vitally united to the apostles in Christ Jesus. This is why those bishops with apostolic succession are truly *catholic:* they are in fact one body with the apostles in the eucharist of the church. But for St. Irenaeus as well as for St. Ignatius, the remarkable thing about apostolic succession that makes it truly significant as a mark of catholicity, is that the bishops who stand in the apostolic succession manifest but one teaching: "The church which is throughout the whole world, holds her origin firm from the apostles, and perseveres in one and the same teaching concerning God and His Son" (*Adv. Haer.* III.12.7, PG 7, cols. 900-901). The explanation for this unity of teaching lies for St. Irenaeus as well as for St. Ignatius in the one eucharist which they all receive: "Our mind (γνώμη) is in accordance (literally, a symphony — σύνφωνος) with the eucharist, and the eucharist establishes our understanding" (*Adv. Haer.* IV.18.5, col. 1028).

received from Christ himself in the church's holy eucharist. The bishop therefore does not constitute the church nor does he determine Christian teaching; he is manifested as a fundamental *mark* of the catholic church only if his teaching is catholic, which it can be only if it derives from the worship of the church's eucharist. In the mind of Christ, that is to say in the worship of the church, in her eucharist, he will teach unwaveringly and in full conviction that Jesus Christ our Lord "is truly of the family of David with respect to human descent, Son of God with respect to the divine will and power, truly born of a virgin, baptized by John in order that all righteousness might be fulfilled by him, truly nailed in the flesh for us under Pontius Pilate and Herod the tetrarch (from his divinely blessed suffering, we derive as its fruit our very existence), in order that he might raise a banner for the ages through his resurrection for his saints and faithful people, whether among Jews or among Gentiles, in the one body of his church."[47]

Those who would be in the catholic church will therefore find those bishops who *prove* their apostolic succession by their teaching. And their teaching will prove its apostolic *catholicity* in that it will agree in all particulars with the teaching concerning Jesus Christ that has characterized the catholic church from the beginning. This teaching, moreover, will bear the fundamental mark of catholicity: it will have the power of divine life; it will be permeated with the fragrance of the church's divine love that emanates from and bears witness to the church's eucharist, the actual substance of the gospel, the fruit of Christ's passion and resurrection, Christ's body and blood, which has destroyed death by his death and given to those who were dead in sin newness of divine life through the drinking of the church's eucharist. United to the bishops of the catholic church, one is united with the church as the church is united with Jesus Christ and Jesus Christ with the Father.[48]

St. Ignatius writes with an intensity and clarity that could only come from a vision of divine ecclesial realities made all the more perceptive by his steadfast resolve to suffer a martyr's death as a concrete witness to the ineffable mercy and love that can be found only in the majesty of the Father Most High and Jesus Christ his only Son.[49] Out of this vision his letters are written with a conviction that at stake is one's very life and eternal destiny. If one succumbs to the seduction of the heresies promulgated by

---

47. *Smyrneans* 1.2.
48. *Ephesians* 5.1.
49. Cf. the salutation of his letter *To the Romans,* and §5.

the contemptible false teachers of this age, one rejects the eucharist of the catholic church, one separates oneself from the catholic bishops of the church, and one turns away from the life-giving blood of Jesus Christ who alone has power over death and who alone can give to man the eternal life in God for which he yearns. In this spirit, St. Ignatius warns: "Be careful, therefore, not to oppose the bishop, for he who is not in the sanctuary with them lacks the bread of God which is the flesh of Christ. . . . These are the last times. Let us fear the patience of God lest it become a judgment against us. Let us fear the wrath to come, or love the grace which is present; only let us be found in Christ Jesus which leads to true life."[50]

Conclusion

The seriousness with which St. Ignatius exhorts those who would be catholic prevents those who claim to love the catholic church from dismissing his teaching as the antiquated opinions of a gray-hair of the church, long since dead. Either we belong to the church of St. Ignatius or we don't, and we do not belong simply by saying we belong. We belong only if we have tasted the love of Jesus Christ, not in *any* eucharist, but in that one true eucharist which is indeed his life-giving body and blood; and we cannot make a true eucharist apart from the catholic bishops of the catholic church, no matter how sophisticated or creative our theological constructions might be. If this is offensive to some, then it is offensive; it still stands, for our wounded pride cannot change it if it is true. We can choose to ignore or reject the eucharistic teaching of St. Ignatius, but we cannot change what he said, just as we cannot make the church of which he was a bishop. We are free to construct any theological system or religious experience that pleases us, but we are not free to escape the consequences of that choice.

Nor are the words of St. Ignatius comfortable for those who seek to heal the schism of Christians by trying to *make* an ecumenical church through theological consensus or convergence. If the full impact of St. Ignatius' teaching were acknowledged, the character of the ecumenical movement would change completely. No longer would we seek to *make* a unified, catholic church, and no longer would we seek to *make* catholic unity by means of a eucharist that *we* construct, which bears witness not to

50. *Ephesians* 5.1. & 11.1.

unity and to the true knowledge of God received from Christ himself, but to ignorance and separation from God by all the conflicting teachings represented by the different confessions that participate in such a eucharist. We would seek to *find* the one, holy, catholic, and apostolic church, and we would draw near in humility, faith, and love to that eucharist which alone is in fact the life-giving body and blood of Jesus Christ, our Lord God and Savior.

But neither can St. Ignatius' eucharistic ecclesiology be considered wholly friendly to those two communions which alone have no need for ecclesiological gymnastics in order to demonstrate the authenticity of their claims to episcopal continuity with the apostles — either on historical or theological grounds. Neither one may be able to sit for long under the sharp scrutiny of its impartial gaze without squirming or casting a downward glance to an embarrassed pair of sandaled feet. The one communion might consider if its ecclesiastical magisterium, in an effort to protect the integrity of the catholic faith, has not in fact replaced the eucharist as *the* criterion of orthodoxy; while in the case of the other apostolic communion, the witness to the concrete, loving unity of the one eucharist which they all claim to possess is betrayed by the administrative chaos generated out of the political pettiness of feuding bishops. A paranoid ethnic parochialism too often has completely shoved the eucharist aside, and reduced the church to an ethnic ghetto or an old-country federation for which a holy, divine eucharist, in which there is neither Jew nor Greek, has no relevance. This heretical phyletism has not only betrayed, but has even killed, the evangelical and missionary spirit of the church. Catholicity proves itself not merely through the physical continuity of apostolic succession, but through the concrete manifestation in word and in deed of the divine life received in the church's eucharist. Those who have been made one body of the one holy catholic and apostolic church cannot destroy the church by their heresy. But, precisely because they are not the church — since Jesus Christ alone is the *ekklesia* and they only have *become ekklesia* by his grace — they cannot lay claim to *being* church when they reduce the catholicity of the church to ethnic and magisterial parochialism, thereby trampling underfoot the precious pearl of divine life they have received in the church's holy eucharist.

In my opinion, no church reformer has ever succeeded in piecing together an ecclesiology with consequences more radical than this eucharistic ecclesiology articulated near the well-spring of the church's historical life. Neither the measures of the reforming popes, nor Luther's justification by grace through faith, nor Calvin's doctrine of predestination, nor Menno Simons' pietism, nor Wesley's devout methodism, nor the attempted conciliarism of the medieval Latin church, succeed as efficiently as St. Ignatius' eucharistic ecclesiology in undercutting completely any human striving or work or authority that would claim to stand as the criterion of orthodoxy or the means to salvation; for in this eucharistic ecclesiology, not even one's faith will save one, since faith in and of itself — as illustrated by the righteous of the Old Testament — is not possessed of the divine life we need to live forever. It is merely the hope that looks for the consummation of its desire in an act of God. That act is his Incarnation, and its fruit is the church's eucharist by which believers may enter into the very accomplishment of God's mighty act by becoming one body with Jesus Christ, not just in theory or in religious imagination or in dogmatic assertion or in credal affirmation, but in reality, in flesh as well as in spirit. Nor will any reformer ever succeed in accomplishing such a radical overhaul of our notion of catholicity and the church, for no reformer can duplicate or make a eucharist that is truly Christ's body and blood simply by saying it is so. No man, no bishop, no preacher, has the power to renew the life of the dead; only the truly catholic church can do that, because she is not simply a community of believers sharing a common faith or religious experience, but she is the very body and blood of Jesus Christ, the only lover of mankind who alone has power over death and darkness.

The Eucharist in the Church

RICHARD A. NORRIS, JR.

This essay will not address the traditional — and thoroughly engaging — Latin and Western puzzles about the mode of Christ's presence in the eucharist or about the sense in which this solemn giving of thanks ought to be qualified by the epithet "sacrificial." Those are important issues, and it is always a pleasure to argue about them; but even important issues can from time to time be, if not unprofitable, then at least out of place. Of more immediate importance for Protestant Christians in North America — and especially perhaps for so-called mainline Protestant groups — is the equally basic question of the practical place of the Lord's Supper in the life of the church; and that is the question to be addressed here, from a point of view that cheerfully mixes theological and historical considerations.

In the traditions we have inherited, no matter how they label themselves or whence they stem, the eucharist, if not always under that name, has classically been central for Christian practice and piety. Yet one gets the impression that nowadays, in the largest portion of American Protestantism, the eucharist is for practical purposes viewed with a certain condescension — the same sort of condescension that members of the House of Lords in Gilbert and Sullivan's *Iolanthe* reserved for the "lower middle classes." It is a phenomenon one is obliged to acknowledge but with which one nevertheless prefers not to be excessively familiar.

There are many reasons, and not just one, for this attitude; and most of them have little, save perhaps marginally, to do with any serious theological stance. The eucharist is a ritual; and by and large Americans do not seem to approve of rituals that are not associated either with marriage ceremonies, the Super Bowl, or Halloween. Further, it is a ritual that attributes spiritual value to physical actions and external things: the taking, blessing, and consuming, that is, of bread and wine; and this seems odd, if not superstitious, to folk who secretly think that "spiritual" is a term undeviatingly synonymous with "intangible and inward" — or, to put the same point in other words, to folk who perceive the enactment of this ritual as a slightly shady violation of the strict boundary between the turf of "science" and that of "religion." And, of course, our attitude also has something to do with the claim that is made about the presence of Jesus in the sacrament; for this claim is bound to appear suspect to people who, in spite of their annual celebrations of Easter, tend to think of Jesus as — to employ a phrase I once heard — "the late J. Christ of biblical fame." They will, consciously or unconsciously, perceive the Lord's Supper as a kind of memorial service;[1] and no normal person is likely to be enthusiastic about the multiplication of funerary observances.

It may be useful, then, just for the sake of contrast, to examine the understanding of the role of the eucharist that by and large governed ancient Christian practice — the practice to which present-day usage must in the end look to discern the roots, and indeed the ultimate logic, of its own observance. What that practice, in its broad outlines, was can be gathered by consulting Justin Martyr's familiar *Apology*, which stems from Rome in the midst of the second century, and which has the advantage, for our purposes, of being relatively early and relatively unsophisticated.

In this work, Justin begins by describing, presumably for the benefit of Emperor Antoninus Pius, the process that people went through to be "dedicated to God" by being "made new in Christ": that is, how they were instructed, and then, after much fasting and praying, were "born again" when they were "washed, calling on the name of God the Father and Master of all, and of our Savior Jesus Christ, and of the Holy Spirit."[2] But the process did not end there: this initiation into the new life in Christ was not completed until the persons thus washed were introduced into the company of "those who are called brethren." There they joined in the community's solemn prayers and in the kiss of peace. They then saw the "presiding officer of the brethren" take bread and a cup of mixed wine and water and heard him send up "praise and glory to the Father of all through the name

---

1. I am not thinking here of what is commonly called "Zwinglianism," which turns, not on the "pastness" of the Christ, but on his present location (i.e., in "heaven").

2. Justin Martyr, *I Apology* 61.1-3.

of the Son and of the Holy Spirit" and "make thanksgiving at considerable length for our being made worthy of these things by him." Justin goes on: "And when he has completed the prayers and the giving of thanks, the entire people in attendance assents by saying *Amen*."[3] There follows, of course, what is nowadays called the communion; and Justin tells us that "this food is called 'eucharist' *(eucharistia)*," and that it "is the flesh and blood of that incarnate Jesus."[4]

Now this is obviously an account of a special occasion: for baptisms, in all probability, did not take place more than two or three times in the course of a year. It is interesting, however, that even on such a special occasion, the culminating act is that of the great thanksgiving, the eucharist, with all that it involves. While the baptisms were going on somewhere close by, the regular body of "the people" *(laos)* was no doubt gathered in the church's house, to hear the reading of the Scriptures and the preaching, while waiting with some modest impatience to be joined by the new set of sharers in Jesus' calling and destiny. But even when there were no baptisms, the church, when it gathered in one place "on the day which is said to belong to the sun," enacted the very same ritual steps: the readings; the presiding officer's *logos* — his "discourse" on the readings; the prayers; the kiss; the bringing forward of bread and wine; the thanksgiving; the sharing out of the "eucharistized" bread and wine.[5] The church's "thing," it would seem, the "thing" that it invariably did at its statutory weekly gathering, was this liturgy that focused successively on the Scriptures and their message; the people's common prayers of petition or intercession; and the Lord's Supper, whose shorthand designation was "thanksgiving."

Our question of course is, *Why was this so?* Why should just this and not some other pattern of actions embody or represent the church's "thing"? Justin does not give a complete answer, but he at least intimates one; and it is not a liturgical answer, but a quasi-theological one that grows out of his explanation of the significance of the first day of the week. The reason why the official gathering of the full church occurs on Sundays, he says, is that the first day of the week is at once the day on which God created the cosmos, "the heaven and the earth," bringing light into being and separating light from darkness, and also the day on which God raised his Christ, the Sun of Righteousness, the new light, from the darkness of

3. *I Apology* 65.1-3.
4. *I Apology* 66.1.
5. *I Apology* 67.1-5.

death.[6] The "thing," then, that the gathered church marks, it seems, might be called the renewal of creation in Christ — a renewal that is not only brought home to believers as they share in the baptism of Christ but also opened to, and lived out by, believers as they participate in this liturgy of the Lord's Day.

Now to be sure, there were some folk who thought this symbolism of the first day a bit pallid, not to say niggling. They would have agreed that the week, the seven "days" of Genesis 1, symbolized — among other things — "the present age," that is to say, "the creation . . . groaning in travail together" as it "waits . . . for the revealing of the sons of God" (cf. Rom. 8:19-22). There is no day, however, in the week so understood that could possibly represent the grandeur of this "thing" that the church celebrated at its regular gatherings. They preferred, therefore, to think of the Christian Sunday as meaning, touching, and conveying something that fell quite outside the ordinary course of things, outside the cosmic "week" and all the business, if you like, of "the present age." They accordingly called this Lord's Day "the eighth day," meaning by that a day that did not even fall within the scope of the ordinary week, but quite transcended it. The church's "thing" was the reign of God, the new age promised by the prophets and actualized in the resurrection of Jesus; and this is what baptism and eucharist in their different ways signified and embodied. To carry out these actions was not only to hear but to accept an invitation to God's eternal wedding feast and to sit, if only momentarily and by anticipation, at the Lord's table. It was to discern, to touch, and to taste the "new thing" that God is bringing about — yes, and to be part of it. This was the sense of the whole of the Sunday liturgy in all its parts: the reading and interpretation of the Scriptures; the confident drawing close to God in prayer; the kiss that anticipated the peace of Paradise; the taking, blessing, and consumption of the bread and wine wherein Christ's "flesh and blood" are shared with and among believers.

Now all this is perfectly understandable, as far as it goes, if one gives it even a moment's thought. Every group, when it gathers formally, gathers to "do its thing." It would be strange to attend the prescribed weekly meeting of a bridge club and to find everyone playing gin rummy; or to visit the United States Senate in session and discover that the president *pro tempore* was napping not through a political debate about some prospective bit of legislation but through, say, a session devoted to sensitivity training. Even if one enjoys a game of gin rummy from time to time, or suspects that the

6. *I Apology* 67.7.

members of the Senate might benefit from some semblance of sensitivity, one would nevertheless judge that such activities were no part of the business for which these groups assembled. By the same token, one presumes that when the church gathers formally on the Lord's Day, it does so to celebrate, or to do, or to communicate the "thing" that it stands for; and what this is, as Justin Martyr suggested many centuries ago, is the realities that are immediately involved in and presupposed by the Christian Passover: the dying of Christ into new life, which is not only the immediate meaning of the ministry, execution, and raising of Jesus but also the ultimate meaning of the liberation of the Hebrew slaves from Egypt and of the joyful repentance of Jesus' followers. Call it, if you like, as I was taught back in the 1950s, "the Christ-event."

There are other terms for this Christian "thing," however; and some of them are, for present purposes, more than a little illuminating. Paul, as we all know, calls it "gospel"; and the word "gospel" names something that has two aspects. "Gospel" means good news announced and *attended to,* on the one hand; but it also presupposes, on the other hand, something that quite objectively *happens.* Indeed, it is because the thing actually happens and makes a difference for the better that it can qualify, when announced and heard, as good news. No doubt that explains why good ideas and high ideals, however edifying or enlightening, do not, in and of themselves, qualify as good news; it is at least in part because they do not actually occur, except, to be sure, notionally. It may also explain why, in early Christianity, other expressions that labeled the Christian "thing" tended to lay stress on the *reality* — the happenedness — of what the gospel announces. We must look at one or two of these, for the simple reason that, precisely because they labeled the Christian "thing," they came to be employed of, or in connection with, the Sunday liturgy that Justin had described, and so convey the church's sense of the meaning of that event.

Take that thoughtful interpreter of Paul, the author of Ephesians. He once — and *only* once, I should add — uses the Greek term *oikonomia* for just this purpose. In normal usage, this word referred, in his day, to the art of running a household; and in ours it has of course been transmogrified into "political economy" or simply "economics." Ephesians, though, employed it in a transferred sense to signify God's *cosmic* housekeeping — that is to say, the policy or the program that God is following with a view to the goal of "summing everything up in Christ" (see Eph. 1:9-10). Our author, in other words, conceived of the whole cosmos, in its total history, as God's "household," and of the divine *oikonomia* as what God is constantly up to in and with this "household." This usage, even though it has, as far as I can tell, only one other instance in the New Testament[7] (and that doubtful), was destined to have a long career in Christian discourse, partly, or perhaps even mostly, because it was liberally employed by Irenaeus in his anti-gnostic polemic. Irenaeus used the word not only to denote the "program" that God follows to complete the creation of humanity after Adam's unfortunate lapse, and therefore, centrally, the incarnation and the work of Christ; but also to define the "story" that is the burden of Scripture and confession, and therefore to delimit the legitimate subjects of theological inquiry. To this day, *oikonomia* is employed, in churches that preserve the Greek tradition, to refer to the second great division of Christian instruction. The first is of course "theology," the teaching about God the Trinity; but the second is "the economy" — everything that goes into understanding God's activity "to us-ward," as people used to say: that is, centrally, the person and work of Christ and the sending of the Spirit. Thus what Ephesians calls "the gospel of your salvation" when it is considered as something *heard* can also be called God's *oikonomia* when considered as a divine policy that is happening, being *carried out,* even now. The *oikonomia* is, then, precisely what the gospel announces, not merely as a past but as a present reality whose fulfillment lies in the future.

But Ephesians also uses another word to the same end — a word that the author takes over directly from Paul. This is the term *mustērion,* or, in English, "mystery"; and what it means is not so much a secret, or a mere puzzle, as something too deep for words to grasp or convey fully. If it is a "secret," the reason is not that it must not be known but that it cannot fully be understood and is, in the end, better experienced and intuited than described. Thus the apostle calls the "hardening" of "part of Israel, until the full number of the Gentiles come in" (Rom. 11:25) a mystery, meaning that he sees Jewish rejection of the gospel — an experienced reality — as a phenomenon he cannot fathom, but which he earnestly believes to be temporary and to serve, in the providence of God, the ultimate purpose of the salvation of all humanity. He also employs the word, however, simply to refer to "the mystery which was kept secret for long ages but is now disclosed" (Rom. 16:25-26); and this mystery, revealed "to bring about the obedience of faith," is surely in substance the same in content as Paul's

---

7. See 1 Tim. 1:4, where *oikonomian* (in spite of the KJV, the RSV, and one uncial MS, which has *oikodomēn*) seems to refer to a subject of study and meditation alternative to "tales and endless genealogies."

"gospel" and what he calls "the preaching of Jesus Christ." That is to say, it is, as Colossians would have it, "the mystery of Christ" (Col. 4:3) or of "Christ in you, the hope of glory" (1:27). Writing to his Corinthian congregation, Paul insists, in the face of claims made by some converts to a special "wisdom," that the message of "Christ crucified," while it may appear to human beings as folly, conveys the deep truth of God because it is that very Christ, the crucified one, who is "the wisdom of God," not to mention "the power of God" (cf. 1 Cor. 1:18-25). Hence, when he counters his opponents with the assertion that he, too, can claim to "speak God's wisdom, hidden in a mystery" (2:7),[8] one can assume that the "mystery" in question is, again, not some gnostic *theōroumenon* but quite simply Christ crucified, with all that that meant and included and implied for Paul. What one gathers from the label "mystery," then, is that there is more than meets the eye to the phenomenon in question; or, to multiply metaphors, that it runs too deep for anything short of hip boots, and that what words can manage to convey of it is a great deal less than is actually there. A mystery is a kind of theological iceberg, revealed and hidden at the same time. It is in this sense that Ephesians can speak of "the mystery of [God's] will," which is "the purpose which he set forth in Christ" (Eph. 1:9), or simply "the mystery of Christ" (3:4). By the time 1 Timothy was written, this usage was established: this letter attributed to Paul characterizes the revelation of the Word of God "in the flesh," with all its consequences, as "the mystery of true religion" (1 Tim. 3:16).[9]

Nor did this usage pass out of fashion with the passing of the second century. To take only one or two late instances, Gregory of Nyssa, in his so-called *Catechetical Oration,* speaks of the Trinity as a "mystery" characterized by "depth" and "ineffability";[10] but he also applies the epithet "mystery of the truth" to what we might call the "career" of Christ, from birth to execution and resurrection, with the implication that this whole "*oikonomia* by which God's Word became human"[11] has something of the inscrutable about it, if only because it becomes the basis upon which God and humanity are reconciled as men and women enter into the death and resurrection of the Word incarnate.

---

8. *Theou sophian en mustēriōi tēn apokekrummenēn:* in the user-friendly paraphrase of the RSV, "a secret and hidden wisdom of God."

9. The RSV translates *to tēs eusebeias mustērion* as "the mystery of our religion"; but *eusebeia* connotes right religion.

10. *Oratio catechetica* 9.

11. *Oratio catechetica* 5.

And this, I judge, is the point at which the word *mustērion* takes on yet another dimension of meaning. From the beginning, it was clear that the wonder and strangeness of this "mystery of true religion" lay partly in the circumstance that the mystery was not a "thing" out there to be gawked at, nor some mere idea or doctrine, but an *oikonomia* that sought to incorporate human persons by the power of the Spirit into the calling and the fate of the Christ, the new Adam, and as such the "first-fruits" of a new humanity. Christian talk of "the mystery," then, had always been self-involving talk, in the sense that the believer could not speak of Christ or of God's "economy" generally without speaking in the same breath of him or herself; for the mystery could, as we have seen, be formulated, from one point of view, simply as "Christ in you, the hope of glory." It is hardly surprising, then, that one should find the same Gregory speaking of "the mystery of new birth," meaning by that, of course, the whole business of baptism. For the "mystery of new birth," as he sees it, is precisely the enactment of an "affinity and likeness" between human believers on the one hand and the "pioneer of our salvation" on the other. The surface symbolism of baptism is one of death with a view to new life, or, alternately stated, burial and resurrection, as the apostle had taught (see Rom. 6:4); and the surface symbolism corresponds, Gregory thinks, with the mystery it expresses: the mystery of Christ crucified and risen as the one in whom our destiny is limned and actualized. To carry out the action of baptism, then, is to participate in the new life of Christ.

This designation of baptism as "mystery" was not peculiar to Gregory; in fact, by his time it was a commonplace. It meant that baptism was an event whose deepest meaning was the death and resurrection of Christ, as one can learn briskly from a younger contemporary of Gregory's who taught in the sphere of the church of Antioch: Theodore, the bishop of Mopsuestia. Theodore observes to a class he is preparing for baptism that life immortal and incorruptible was first actualized "for us" by "our Lord Jesus Christ, who was assumed" into union with the divine Word "from among us." When, therefore, we "carry out this mystery, which contains the incomprehensible signs of the divine 'economy' with respect to Christ," it is in the certain knowledge that what came to pass for Christ shall also come to pass for us.[12] Theodore passes on, however, to remark that the Lord's Table is also, and in the same sense, a mystery — a presentation, in-

---

12. R. Tonneau, ed. and trans., *Les homélies catéchétiques de Théodore de Mopsueste* (Vatican City, 1949), p. 331.

deed, of the mystery of Christ crucified, carried out with signs and types, so that by participating in this mystery "we obtain possession of the good things to come together with the remission of sins."[13] Like baptism, then, the eucharist was perceived as a thing *carried out,* performed; and precisely this action was a "mystery" in the sense that it was the tip of the iceberg called "God's *oikonomia*" — that what was "done" or carried out in it was an *expression* or "type" of the dying and resurrection of the Christ.

And so we come to the word *sacramentum,* "sacrament." It is a matter of common knowledge by now that this Latin term was habitually employed by Christians in North Africa to translate the Greek *mustērion* as that term occurred in the Septuagint and the New Testament. The reasons for this are both obscure and, as far as we know them, peculiarly unsatisfying. The fact is that *sacramentum* was a word that early came to be used for almost any sacred and obligatory bond, and in particular for the military oath of allegiance taken by recruits to the Roman army — an oath that was therefore regarded as sacred and unbreakable. When Greek-speakers sought an equivalent word for this military oath, they — or some of them — lit upon *mustērion,* perhaps because it, too, had overtones of the sacred and solemn; and it is here, presumably, that the association of these two words began. It is difficult, I grant, to see how a mind might leap from this particular sense of *sacramentum* to the range of meanings it assumed as a general equivalent for *mustērion.* Nevertheless *sacramentum* became established for this purpose before the date of any nonbiblical writings we have in the Latin tongue. It had its own special connotations, to be sure. Just as *mustērion* always carried an overtone of something unfathomable, *sacramentum* inevitably carried associations of the sacred, just as it carried — especially when applied to baptism — the connotation of an oath, a self-commitment or "pact." To put the matter in another way, *mustērion* suggests a reality — and specifically, the *oikonomia* of God — which, even though one inevitably speaks of oneself in speaking of it, can be characterized only haltingly and inadequately; while *sacramentum* for its part almost inevitably suggests an encounter with another "party" — that is, it presupposes an engagement of some sort that involves self-commitment.

"Gospel," "mystery," "sacrament" — these are all classical terms for the *oikonomia* of God, focally and definitively worked out in the destiny of the "body" of Christ: death to sin and new life with God, that "life of the age to come" of which the creed speaks. Through the lenses provided by

13. Tonneau, ed., p. 473.

these words one can, moreover, take a fresh squint at Justin's first-day —
or eighth-day — liturgy, so as to grasp its sense more fully and exactly by
looking at it from a different angle.

The first thing, then, is to dwell briefly on that word *oikonomia* and
to grasp the implication of the fact that it refers, roughly speaking, to *what
God is up to with us;* and further, that this *what God is up to* encompasses
past and future as well as present. One cannot think or speak about it without reference, tacit or explicit, to creation and its purpose, the giving of the
Law, the testimony of the prophets, the ministry and death and resurrection of Jesus. By the same token, one cannot bring it to mind without ad-
verting to the coming fulfillment of God's purpose: the state of affairs that
Jesus called "the reign of God," which was instantiated in his resurrection,
and which for us is real as the subject of confident hope. Here is a reality
that is at the same time unfinished: a thing God does, has been doing, and
will be doing; and into the doing of which God incorporates us by faith.
Unfinished or not, however, its "sense" is revealed: what God is up to is
"summed up," as Irenaeus of Lyon used to say, in the life, death, and resurrection of the Word incarnate; and so the church when it gets together can
think of nothing better to do than to celebrate this reality in which the
mystery of God's will — to employ a useful figure — surfaces.

The celebration of it — and that, of course, as need hardly be said, is
what Justin's Sunday liturgy is — is itself a mystery, as the ancient church
rightly understood. That is to say, it is a secondary and dependent surfacing of the underlying mystery of *what God is up to with us,* and this in two
humanly executed modes of presentation. The first is the mode of proclamation, in which the mystery, apprehended as gospel, is rehearsed in
speaking and obedient hearing as the Scriptures are read and explicated.
This, it must be emphasized, is a human action, forever inadequate to the
mystery that, by God's grace, surfaces in it, but nevertheless an intimation
and celebration of it — and more than that, an engagement with it. Presented thus as gospel, Christ in his ministry, death, resurrection, and coming is set forth as *what God is up to with us,* or better, perhaps, *what God intends with us;* and our response is *faith,* hopeful faith that cannot resist a
certain anxious — and (alas!) occasional — indulgence in love.

In Justin's liturgy, however, the mystery surfaced also in a second
manner: in the taking of bread and wine, the giving thanks over them, the
breaking of the bread, and the sharing of the broken bread and outpoured
wine, the assembled church symbolically *acted out* the mystery — that is,
the *oikonomia* of the ministry, death, resurrection, and coming of the in-

carnate Word. These actions were, of course, imitations in a new setting of the remembered actions of Jesus at the Last Supper, and the significance they bore was the significance he had given them. Jesus' words and deeds appear to have constituted a sort of prophetic sign: they were immediate expressions, occurring beforehand, of the Lord's dying into new life; or perhaps it would be better to say that they embodied his death as the ground of a "new covenant," a new relationship between God and God's human creatures, which would be fulfilled in the new age that God in Christ was bringing. In the Last Supper, then, Jesus showed his disciples how to *act out* the mystery of God's purpose for them — how to participate in it by letting his body and his life be theirs; how to live out in symbolic action the calling and the destiny that in Christ are theirs. And this, too, is a mystery in the sense that it is a surfacing of the foundational mystery, a symbolic presentation *in action* of *what God is up to with us*, and therefore, in the way of proper symbolic presentations, a genuine participation in it. It is rather like the "dancing" of a child who waltzes while standing on the feet of a parent: it is both a symbolic and a real dancing to the rhythm which is God's "economy" revealed in Christ.

And therefore this eucharist, taken in its totality, is a "sacrament" in two senses. First of all it is a sacrament in the ancient sense of an act of commitment. Christian faith is after all at its heart a relationship of God with human beings: a relationship founded upon the work of Christ and sustained through the power of the Spirit. This relationship has traditionally been called "New Covenant," and the Latin fathers, Augustine not the least of them, referred to it as a "pactum" — which word might easily be rendered as "contract." As they understood it, the covenant with God in Christ was entered by the gate of baptism; the eucharist, for its part, was the covenant's regular renewal and reiteration, done (save in Lent, to be sure) with alleluias in praise of God's gift. Greek writers of course knew nothing of any *pactum;*[14] but they did understand that the confession of faith made at one's baptism, together with the "down payment" of the Spirit there given, created a new relationship with God — a relationship in which, as Paul had insisted, believers were "clothed" in Christ and so assumed the role of children to God. Thus baptism "stamped" the believer with a new identity in Christ; and it was this identity which the eucharist, through the invoked power of the Spirit, renewed and reiterated.

---

14. See, e.g., Theodore of Mopsuestia, *Homily XV,* in Tonneau, ed., p. 463. Christ's sacrifice on the cross, entered into in the eucharist, is that in which the New Covenant consists.

But in the second place, the eucharist is a "sacrament" in the sense that it, too, is a "mystery." Theodore of Mopsuestia defined "mystery" — *raza'* — as "the presentation in signs and symbols of things invisible and ineffable."[15] Augustine, as is well enough known, also saw what we call "the sacraments" as a species of *signs,* and signs, when they took the form of human gestures or words, were, he insisted, means of communication — means by which one person could enter into the will and feelings of another.[16] They were, in other words, not mere pointers, but ways of entering into something, just as Theodore's "mysteries" were modes of participation in the invisible and ineffable.

Moreover, what was here entered into was precisely *what God is up to with us.* The eucharist, then, is God's taking us on in Christ, assigning us a participation in his body as our destiny and calling. That it is done as *sacramentum,* as *mustērion,* means that it is the real thing, but in the form, if you please, of a preliminary rehearsal, like a tentative performance of the last act of *Hamlet.* Yet it is no small thing to stage, in liturgy and in life: a *sign,* a dress rehearsal, of the reign of God. Everyone knows it is only a rehearsal. The full reality is yet to come. Such a rehearsal, however, is more than a "mark" of the church. It is what the church is.

---

15. *Homily XII,* in Tonneau, ed., p. 325.
16. See, e.g., *De doctrina christiana* II.2.3.

The Office of the Keys:
On the Disappearance of Discipline
in Protestant Modernity

DAVID S. YEAGO

I. Setting the Stage

I want to begin with the text which has apparently inspired this whole conference, and allow Martin Luther to define more closely the shape of my assigned theme.[1] The text in question is, of course, the discussion of the distinguishing characteristics of the church in Luther's 1539 treatise *On the Councils and the Church;* there Luther deals with the office of the Keys in fourth place, immediately following the preaching of the gospel and the celebration of baptism and the Lord's Supper. The citation is lengthy but crucial to our purpose:

> Fourth, one recognizes the people of God or the holy Christian people by the Keys, which they exercise publicly, as Christ institutes in Matthew 18, so that when a Christian sins, he is disciplined, and if he does not improve, he is to be bound and cast out. If he does improve, he is to be absolved. These are the Keys. Now there is a twofold exercise of the Keys, public and private. For there are some people who are so weak and depressed in their conscience that even if they have not been publicly condemned, they cannot take comfort until they have received absolution

---

1. Translations of Luther are my own from *D. Martin Luther's Werke. Kritische Gesamtausgabe* (Weimar, 1883ff.), cited as *WA*. I will provide reference where possible to the English translation in *Luther's Works* (Concordia & Fortress, 1955-), cited as *LW*.

privately from the pastor. On the other hand, there are others who are so obstinate that neither in their heart nor in the presence of the pastor do they want to be forgiven or to cease from sinning. Therefore the exercise of the Keys must proceed in both ways, public and private. Now, where you see that sin is being forgiven or disciplined in certain persons, publicly or privately, there you know that the people of God is present, for where the people of God is absent the Keys are also absent, and where the Keys are absent, the people of God is also absent. For Christ left the Keys as a legacy, to be a public sign and holy thing through which the Holy Spirit (acquired by Christ's death) might sanctify fallen sinners anew, and through which Christians might confess that they are a holy people subject to Christ in this world. Those who do not want to be converted or to be sanctified anew, are cast out from this holy people, that is, bound and excluded by the Keys, as happened to the impenitent Antinomians.[2]

Perhaps contrary to our expectations, Luther does not present the office of the Keys here with the emphasis on the Key of absolution, as primarily an office of consolation. On the contrary, he leads with the Key of binding; that is, the issue of the Keys is the public discipline of the Christian community, the corporate response of the holy people to the sins of its members. The issue of consolation arises within this communal context: there will be tender souls who, as it were, *anticipate* the Key of binding and condemn themselves in the privacy of their own hearts; for these the Key of absolution can likewise be exercised in private. But this presupposes a public discipline, in which open sin is met with open reproof and resistance, and impenitence has public consequences; it presupposes, as Luther wrote a page earlier, at the conclusion of his discussion of the eucharist, that *"the church or people of God does not suffer public sinners in its midst, but disciplines them and makes them holy as well, or else, if they will not agree, it casts them out of the holy place through the ban, and regards them as Gentiles."*[3] Such public discipline, Luther insists, is a distinguishing mark of the Christian church: *"where you see that sin is being forgiven or disciplined . . . publicly or privately, there you know that the people of God is present, for where the people of God is absent the Keys are also absent, and where the Keys are absent, the people of God is also absent."*

For many of us, I suspect, it will be difficult to decide which is the greater shock in this passage, what is being said or the fact that it is Luther

2. *WA* 50:631-32; cf. *LW* 41:153.
3. *WA* 50:631; *LW* 41:152-53.

who is saying it. On the one hand, if this sort of corporate discipline is, as Luther says, an invariant and essential sign or "mark of the Body of Christ," then what shall we say about mainline Protestant Christianity at this end of the twentieth century? We have difficulty, surely, in recognizing ourselves in this depiction of what is essential to the church, and Luther sets the stakes of such non-recognition very high: *"where the Keys"* — understood as a public practice of reproof and reconciliation — *"are absent, the people of God is also absent."* Is the kingdom then to be taken away from us and given to the Gentiles — to the fundamentalists and papists and others who fit this description far more clearly than we?

On the other hand, how can it be Luther, *Luther* of all people, who presents us with this provocation? One expects this sort of thing from the *Schwärmer,* or from Calvin, or the more dour church fathers — but not from the great Reformer, the supposed rediscoverer of the radically law-free Pauline gospel, whose view of church-fellowship has been set forth under the title *"Community without Conditions."*[4] To find Luther saying *this* sort of thing, and to realize that this is no isolated outbreak, but his consistent and considered position, is surely for many of us to have a whole network of assumptions about the meaning of the Reformation called into question. But that brings us back to the first shock that Luther's words induce, for at the heart of this web of assumptions is a central assumption that *we* — we mainline Christians of the late twentieth century — are the legitimate heirs of Luther's reform, that our "inclusive" churches and our relaxed mode of common life are what the great Reformation had in view, over against what we are pleased to regard as Roman authoritarianism, Orthodox obscurantism, and evangelical Protestant sectarianism.

I want to let this twofold provocation guide us further, and in particular, to let the second shed light on the first; that is, I want to start from our sense that we do not recognize the Luther who says such things, and let that be a point of entry to a clearer understanding of our situation in the so-called mainline Protestant churches today.[5] If Luther can say such

---

4. Cf. Hermann Kleinknecht, *Gemeinschaft ohne Bedingungen: Kirche und Rechtfertigung in Luther's grosser Galaterbrief-Vorlesung von 1531* (Calwer, 1981).

5. I will freely stipulate that the so-called "mainline" churches are now sociologically "oldline" if not "sideline." Nevertheless, "mainline" remains a useful designation, not only because it is familiar, but because it still expresses the self-understanding of these churches. I hope that these reflections are also useful to Roman Catholics, Orthodox, and evangelical Protestants, but it would be presumptuous of me to address directly the state of church discipline in their communities.

things, then there must be underlying beliefs and understandings at work which were obvious to him but have in the meantime become opaque to us. In particular, I believe, this is the case at two points adumbrated in a summary sentence in the text with which we began: *"For Christ left the Keys as a legacy, to be a public sign and holy thing through which the Holy Spirit (acquired by Christ's death) might sanctify fallen sinners anew, and through which Christians might confess that they are a holy people subject to Christ in this world."* The office of the Keys thus plays a double role: it serves the *Spirit's* work of sanctifying the fallen, and at the same time plays a part in the *church's* mission of confession before the world. To measure the distance that separates us from Luther, therefore, we must look to these two themes: holiness and its relationship to the gospel of grace, on the one hand, and the mission of the church in the world, on the other.

II. The Keys, Holiness, and the Witness of the Christian People

Holiness is an insistent and pervasive theme of the ecclesiology of *On the Councils and the Church;* the text is saturated with the language of sanctification, consecration, and divine anointing.[6] The church is a public assembly, as tangible as a town meeting, but by virtue of the special summons which assembles this people, it is no common gathering "but *sancta Catholica Christiana,* that is, a Christian holy people."[7] The seven marks of the church are the *Heilthümer,* according to Luther, the holy things, by which this holy people is sanctified. The expression actually involves an untranslatable play on words: *Heilthum* in Luther's world meant a miracle-working relic, a sacred object bursting with divine power. The true wonder-working holy things, Luther is claiming, are the seven elements of communal life which he describes: the word of God, baptism, the sacrament of the altar, the office of the Keys, the holy ministry, the public liturgy of prayer, praise, and thanksgiving, and the bearing of the holy cross. These are the instruments of the Spirit, through which he makes the people of God a *holy* Christian people.

Furthermore, Luther is at pains to make clear what he means by holi-

---

6. For a broader treatment of Luther's ecclesiology, and of this treatise in particular, cf. my essay, "A Christian, Holy People: Martin Luther on Salvation and the Church," *Modern Theology* 13 (1997): 101-20.

7. *WA* 50:624; *LW* 41:143.

ness; it is emphatically not a merely dialectical holiness grounded only forensically, in divine imputation. On the contrary, he insists explicitly that the Spirit sanctifies Christians "not only by the forgiveness of sins, which Christ has gained for them (as the Antinomians teach) but also by the putting-away, the purging-out, and the putting-to-death of sins. . . ."[8] The credal confession of the holy church means that "there always exists on earth in this life a Christian holy people in which Christ lives, works, and rules *per redemptionem,* through grace and the forgiveness of sins, and the Holy Spirit *per vivificationem & sanctificationem,* through daily cleansing-out of sins and renewal of life, so that we do not remain in sins, but can and should lead a new life in all kinds of good works and not in the old, evil works, as the Ten Commandments or two tables of Moses enjoin."[9]

Luther then goes on to look at Christian holiness in detail as the fulfillment of the two tables of the Decalogue. Through the word the Spirit imparts true knowledge of God, and with it confidence and courage, reverence, love, and thankfulness towards God. "This means a new holy life in the soul in accord with the first table of Moses. It is also called 'the three theological virtues,' the three main virtues of a Christian, faith, hope, and love."[10] This renewal of the soul is matched, however, by a new life for the *body;* here, as so often in Luther, talk of "the body" refers to what is *public,* to concrete presence in the public world of social interaction and exchange. Thus sanctification of the body for Luther involves not only the sixth commandment and sexual morality; it involves the whole range of our concrete social relationships as well, thus issues about authority and violence and possessions and language, the matter of the remaining commandments. The Spirit who renews the heart also brings the Christian people to a visibly renewed pattern of life in the public world, marked by respect for due authority, renunciation of interpersonal violence, chastity and sexual discipline, honesty and generosity in dealing with possessions, and truthful gentleness of speech.

This new way of being present in the bodily world, in obedience to the second table of Moses, is for Luther a kind of beginning of the bodily resurrection: "This is the work of the Holy Spirit, who sanctifies and awakens the body also to a new life of this sort, until it is fulfilled in the life to come."[11] Luther is quite aware that such newness of life is anything but a

8. *WA* 50:624; *LW* 41:143.
9. *WA* 50:625; *LW* 41:144.
10. *WA* 50:626; *LW* 41:146.
11. *WA* 50:627; *LW* 41:146.

matter of course; it is an article of faith that there must be *some* such holy people in the world, but he makes the rueful suggestion that they may all, at a given moment, be children: "Alas, old people like that are few." Nonetheless, he refuses to retreat from his insistence that such inner and outer renewal of life is non-negotiable, not simply something which should but may not follow from faith, but part of what it means to have faith: "Those who are not like that should not consider themselves Christians, and one should not console them with a lot of chatter about the forgiveness of sins and the grace of Christ, as though they were Christians, as the Antinomians do."[12]

Let me try to formulate what lies behind a statement like this, in truth common enough in Luther's work, yet so shockingly out of harmony with our expectations: for Luther, God's justifying act through the gospel is an act by which he graciously *accomplishes* his holy will, the very same will that is declared gracelessly in the law. In Luther's preaching and teaching, the main stress is to be sure of the *graciousness* of this act: in justification, God accomplishes his will by *giving* us freely what his law demands, indeed by giving us his only Son to be our righteousness. The gospel, the word in which God declares and executes this gracious giving, thus brings consolation to the weak and trembling conscience, hope to the struggler, encouragement to the downhearted. But however powerful the motive of consolation, it is never simply absolute. What the gospel declares and executes is always the *fulfillment* of God's commandments, never their suspension:

> Now when Christ condemns all works of the law, and demands that the person must first be blessed and good, it might appear as though he were condemning good works and dissolving all law, yet he is really teaching us for the first time how to do good works. Therefore he speaks against such complaints and says: "You shall not complain that I am come to dissolve the law. I desire rather to fulfill it through faith in me. . . ."[13]

Faith's confidence, therefore, is always confidence that Christ will indeed carry out his design, that through his reign over us, the will of the Father *shall* be accomplished in us and indeed by us, in conflict with the world,

12. *WA* 50:627; *LW* 41:147.
13. *WA* 10/I/1:359. Cf. J. N. Lenker, *Sermons of Martin Luther* (Grand Rapids: Baker Book House, 1983), vol. 6, p. 250.

the flesh, and the devil. In the midst of such conflict, the gospel is consolation and assurance; but to those who would hold back from the struggle, Luther does not believe that there is any honest word of consolation to be spoken, except the very word that would summon them to the battle: "Christ will be *your* Lord, and you may live under his rule and serve him!" Justification is therefore not a sheer forensic acceptance which changes nothing and must somehow be followed by a separate work of sanctification. For Luther, *justification sanctifies;* it is a divine act by which the whole human being, body and soul, falls under the sway of the righteous reality of Jesus Christ, crucified and risen.

It is for this reason that Luther does not regard the proclamation of the gospel as a pure discourse of consolation and promise. Gospel proclamation also includes the necessary moment which Luther, following the medieval Latin pastoral tradition, refers to as *admonition* or *exhortation:*

> The office of preaching is necessary in the church not only for the ignorant who need to be taught, such as the simple, unreflective crowd and the young people, but also for those who know very well how they should believe and live, in order to awaken and admonish them to be on guard daily and not become lazy, downhearted, and weary in the struggle which they must carry on in this world against the devil, their own flesh, and all sorts of vices.[14]

What follows makes it clear that this admonition is not in essence a reversion from gospel to law, but rather a necessary dimension of the gospel which sustains faith:

> [Paul] knows that even though Christians have begun to believe, and are in a condition in which the fruits of faith should prove themselves, yet this is not automatically forthcoming. It won't do at this point to say and think: "Yes, that's enough, the doctrine has been given to them, now the fruits and the good works will follow by themselves." For even though the Spirit is present and (as Christ says) is willing and is at work in those who believe, yet on the other hand the flesh is also present, and it is weak and lazy, and in addition, the devil never takes a vacation from his effort to ruin this weak flesh through tribulation and seduction.[15]

14. *WA* 22:312; cf. Lenker, vol. 8, p. 305.
15. *WA* 22:312; Lenker, vol. 8, p. 305.

The exhortation to a new life insistently presses on faith the full dimensions precisely of God's free gift in Christ. That gift cannot be received all at once — it is too great and our hearts are too puny for that; it must be constantly received more and more by faith in the midst of the struggle with the world, the flesh, and the devil.

But of course, when gospel admonition is not heeded, when it runs up against self-deception, willfulness, and the stubborn torpor of the flesh, it does indeed shade into accusing law; it becomes a word of *warning and judgment* that exposes and resists the abuse of gospel freedom and insists on the binding force of Paul's apostolic death-sentence: "If you live according to the flesh, you must die" (Romans 8:13). Luther comments:

> Christ certainly did not die for those who intend to remain in their sins; he died to rescue from their sins those who would gladly be released but cannot liberate themselves. Therefore, let a Christian not be impressed with this nonsense: I am free from the Law, therefore I may do what I want. But say and do the opposite: because you are a Christian, fear and shun sin, lest you move from freedom back to the earlier bondage to sin under the law and God's wrath, and fall from the life that you began back into death. For here stands the serious judgment: "If you live according to the flesh, you will die." It is as though the apostle wanted to say: It will not help you that you hear the Gospel, that you boast of Christ, that you receive the sacraments, so long as you do not, through the faith and the Holy Spirit you have received, quench the sinful desires of your godlessness, your contempt for God, your greed, malice, pride, hatred, envy, and so on.[16]

In all this, Luther stands in a tradition of pastoral theology that goes back at least to Gregory the Great's *De regula pastorali,* which should be translated *On Pastoral Governance.* In Gregory's vision, pastors govern the flock of Christ with the word of admonition: the skilled shepherd must know how to speak to all the different types of sheep in the flock, to keep them all moving, the strong and the weak, the wise and the foolish, the powerful and the insignificant, towards the goal of the heavenly calling.[17] Luther's pastoral theology of law and gospel should be read as a develop-

---

16. *WA* 22:133; Lenker, vol. 8, pp. 169-70.
17. On Gregory the Great, cf. Carole Straw, *Gregory the Great: Perfection in Imperfection* (Berkeley: University of California Press, 1988).

ment of the Gregorian model: the skilled shepherd must know when to comfort, when to exhort, when to give warning, and when to pronounce judgment. Furthermore, of course, Luther insists that the whole struggle of the Christian people be carefully understood as a struggle over which *grace* presides: we do not strive anxiously to win God's favor but seek joyfully to receive his gift, despite the seduction and contempt of the world, the laziness and timidity of the flesh, and the fury and deceit of the devil. Yet with Gregory and the whole tradition, Luther insists that the free gift is the *accomplishment* of God's holy will in us and by us; the gift has therefore not truly been given until we begin to *live* and not die. As he puts it in a sermon on Colossians 3, for Easter Wednesday:

> What help is it to a dead man, however much you preach to him about life, if he does not come alive as a result? Or about righteousness to a sinner if he remains in sin? Or about truth to an erring, sectarian spirit if he does not cease from his error and darkness? Even so, it is not only pointless but harmful and destructive to hear about the glorious and blessed comfort of the resurrection if the heart never experiences it, but there remains only the sound of it in the ears, or a froth of it on the tongue, and nothing more comes of it than among those who have never heard of it. For this admirable work and precious treasure of Christ's resurrection, Paul wants to say, must not be a useless, inert, and impotent chatter or idea . . . but a power and energy which through faith works a resurrection in us too, which he calls rising with Christ, that is, dying to sin, being snatched from the power of death and hell, and having life and consolation in Christ.[18]

It is in this context that Luther regards the Keys as an instrument of the sanctifying work of the Spirit. The exercise of the Key of binding is the *ultima ratio* of pastoral governance, the last and most serious word of warning and judgment. The church has been given no power of coercion, only the word, and the Key of binding is the most emphatic utterance of God's "No" to sin at the church's disposal. Precisely as such, it is an instrument of the Spirit, law in the service of gospel, a sharp and biting assault on arrogance and sloth and self-delusion. Thus Luther insists, in his 1530 treatise *On the Keys*, that both the Key of binding and the Key of absolution are "indescribably precious treasures and jewels for our souls":

---

18. *WA* 21:266; Lenker, vol. 7, p. 218.

For the Key which binds carries forward the work of the law. It is profitable to the sinner inasmuch as it reveals to him his sins, admonishes him to fear God, causes him to tremble, and moves him to repentance, and not to destruction. . . . It serves as a wholesome medicine and has a beneficial effect on evil persons, although it is terrifying and annoying to the flesh. . . . For the dear Man, the faithful Bishop of our souls, Jesus Christ, is well aware that his beloved Christians are frail, that the devil, the flesh, and the world would tempt them unceasingly, and in many ways, and that at times they would fall into sin. Therefore, he has given us this remedy, the Key which binds, so that we might not remain too confident in our sins, arrogant, barbarous, and without God, and the Key which looses, that we should not despair in our sins. Thus aided we should stay on a middle road, between arrogance and faint-heartedness, in genuine humility and confidence, being provided for richly in every way.[19]

However, this is not the whole story, for Luther clearly does not envision the use of the Key of binding against any and all sinfulness among Christians, but only what he calls "public" sin. Thus in *On the Councils* he writes that the presence of false and unbelieving Christians in the midst of the church "does not defile the people of God, so long as they are concealed, for the church or people of God does not tolerate public sinners in its midst."[20] The public exercise of the Keys is therefore not only an instrument of the Spirit's work of sanctification directed towards the individual sinner; it also has another dimension, a public dimension, which Luther indicates when he says that the Keys are *"a public sign and holy thing . . . through which Christians may confess that they are a holy people subject to Christ in this world."*[21]

Here we run up against an operative assumption which is not so much a theme as a presupposition of Luther's thought, an element in his faith more than a topic on which his theological work focused. It is the ancient biblical conviction, inherited from Israel, that the people of God is gathered to be a public sign of his glory, that God's name is either hallowed or profaned among the nations by what goes on in the life of his people. This is not, admittedly, the issue on which Luther's ecclesiology is concentrated, but it is always present in the bedrock of his assumptions, and comes occasionally to memorable expression, as

19. *LW* 40:372-73.
20. *WA* 50:631; *LW* 41:152
21. *WA* 50:632; *LW* 41:153.

for example in the *Large Catechism* exposition of the first petition of the Lord's Prayer:

> But how does [God's name] become holy among us? Answer, in as plain terms as possible: When both our teaching and life are godly and Christian. For since we call God our Father in this prayer, we are obligated always to conduct ourselves and present ourselves as devoted children, so that he may not receive shame but honor and praise from us.[22]

The greatest profanation of God's name is false teaching in the church, but close behind comes the dishonor he is done by "an openly evil life and works, when those who are called Christians and God's people are adulterers, drunkards, greedy bellies, envious, and slanderers."

> Here again God's name must meet with shame and be blasphemed on account of us. For just as it is a shame and dishonor to a bodily father to have a wicked spoiled child who contradicts him in words and deeds, so that on account of that child he is looked down on and belittled, so also it redounds to God's dishonor when we, who are called by His name and have received all kinds of good things from Him, teach, speak, and live otherwise than as devoted and heavenly children, so that it is said of us that we must be not God's children, but the devil's.[23]

There are deep subterranean connections between this theme and the notion of the sanctification of the body — connections which Luther himself does not bring fully into the light. God's saving action culminates, not in salvation merely for souls, but in the resurrection of the body, because the ultimate object of God's action is the assertion of his life-giving dominion over the whole creation. Just so, God's anticipation of the final fulfillment in justification must embrace the *bodily* sanctification of his people, that is, a transformed mode of public, bodily presence in the world, as an anticipation of the resurrection of the body and a sign of God's universal rule. The goal of the gospel ministry is therefore not reached until something happens *in public,* out in the world of bodies and embodied social interaction: the sanctification of the people of God in a new "bodily" way of life that glorifies God and proclaims Jesus Christ as Lord.

22. *Die Bekenntnisschriften der evangelisch-lutherischen Kirche,* 11th edition (Göttingen: Vandenhoeck & Ruprecht, 1992), p. 671. Hereafter cited as *BSELK.*
23. *BSELK,* p. 671.

It is for this reason that the church must be concerned with the integrity of its own common life, and such concern may not be dismissed as nothing but pharisaical self-righteousness. The church exists to represent before the nations the gracious governance of the crucified and risen Christ, by which the holy will of the Father is accomplished in the Spirit; in this way the praise and honor of the Triune God are made known upon the earth. Luther sees more acutely than most that God's glory is not denied when the weak are treated gently and forgiveness is extended to the penitent seventy times seven times; such long-suffering rather honors and attests the graciousness with which God seeks to accomplish his holy will among us. But the glory of God *is* denied and falsified when his mercy is abused as a cover for evil-doing and those who are called his children live rather as the children of the devil. Then the church becomes a false and deceiving sign; in effect, its public life sets forth the devil's dominion and says to the world: "Look, this is the reign of Christ the Lord."

III. Between Luther and Ourselves: God and the Disengaged Self

As we turn to measure the distance that separates us from Luther on this issue, the chief difficulty is knowing where to begin, for nearly everything distinctively modern about modern forms of Christianity conspires to alienate us from the tradition in which Luther stood and which he received in his own distinctive way. Indeed, one could write a full-fledged history of the modern transmutation of Christianity from the perspective of this theme, as the story of how the very idea of a public discipline of common life gradually became unthinkable in those western churches that most fully exposed themselves to modernity.[24] Such an account would, of course, also have at least to consider whether the practices of corporate discipline in those western Christian communities that have retained them have not likewise undergone gradual but significant changes of form and function. This paper can't even begin to sketch the dimensions of such a project; but perhaps it is possible to identify two crucial points — there

24. For a sketch of such a telling of the story of Christianity in the modern age, cf. William T. Cavanaugh, "'A Fire Strong Enough to Consume the House': The Wars of Religion and the Rise of the Modern State," *Modern Theology* 11 (1995). I would, however, suggest that the presentation of Luther in this fine essay is a little one-sided.

may, of course, be others of equal significance — at which our underlying assumptions have become quite different from Luther's.

A first point of contrast can perhaps best be brought to light in terms of the concept of *freedom*. In the Lutheran world, at any rate, the summary of the gospel that comes most naturally today is undoubtedly something like this: "Good news! You are free — you don't have to do anything!" The notion of freedom is essentially negative: release from pressure, the lifting of the burden of an unendurable expectation. Compare this with the way Luther speaks of liberation in the *Large Catechism:*

> What does it mean to "become a Lord"? It means that he has liberated me from sin, from the devil, from death, and from all misfortune. For previously I had no Lord or king, but was imprisoned under the devil's power, condemned to death, and ensnared in sin and blindness.[25]

Here, in a most unmodern way, freedom is simply equated with having a Lord and king. The opposition between freedom and bondage is essentially a contrast between good governance and bad; freedom is not construed in such a way that all governance amounts to a compromise with servitude. Thus the appropriate summary of Luther's gospel might go like this: "Good news! You are free — you get to have *Jesus* for your Lord!" Or as Luther himself puts it in the *Large Catechism:*

> Now those tyrants and jailers have been driven away, and their place has been taken by Jesus Christ, a Lord of life, righteousness, all goodness and beatitude, and he has snatched us poor lost human beings from the jaws of hell, claimed *(gewonnen)* us, set us free, and brought us back into the Father's favor and grace, and taken us under his shield and protection as his own property, so that he rules over us by his righteousness, wisdom, power, life, and beatitude.[26]

Note the provocative equations Luther makes, as though they were a matter of course. Freedom cannot mean that the throne of the tyrants and jailers is left empty; another must take their place. We are set free precisely when we are "claimed" by a Lord and King, indeed taken "as his own property." Luther can speak of freedom in this way, I would suggest, because he

---

25. *BSELK*, p. 651. The German text has *er hat erlöset mich*, which would normally be translated "he has redeemed me," but the Latin has *me liberavit*, showing that the original connection of "redemption" with liberation from slavery was still alive for Luther.

26. *BSELK*, p. 652.

is proceeding from two deeply Augustinian assumptions. First, our lives have a purpose, a *telos,* which is *given* to us, given with our very existence, and therefore not chosen or devised by us. Real freedom must therefore always be freedom *for* that goal, *for* that end. But second, this *telos* of our existence is *beyond our scope;* we exist for the sake of an end that we cannot reach by any exercise of creaturely power. If these two assumptions hold good — if our existence has an innate directedness towards a goal that exceeds our grasp — then indeed we will find ourselves free only when we live under a dominion which can actually bring us to that goal.

Thus because Israel only exists as a people in order to be a kingdom of priests, a holy nation before the LORD, yet Israel cannot become such a kingdom and nation by sheer will power, or by any innate competence; therefore Israel's *liberation* is to come under the LORD's dominion, to become his personal property (cf. Exodus 19:3-6). Not only Exodus, therefore, but also Sinai; not only the shattering of Pharaoh's oppressive power but also the LORD God's enthronement, must be intrinsic to what Israel means by freedom. It is not enough to drive out the tyrants and jailers; some new dominion must take their place, some governance capable of bringing about the correspondence of Israel's existence with her calling.

The central move in traditional Christian theological anthropology was to assert that Israel's particular destiny figured the destiny of the whole human race, and of every man and woman: the vocation to priesthood and holiness, and therefore to God's friendship and service, is inscribed in the being of every human person. Thus the commandments given to Israel are read as "natural law" written in every heart; they articulate the "law of our being," the eschatological intentionality of the Creator's act. But the Decalogue, even when read as "natural law," is by no means a lowest common denominator, an ethical minimum; on the contrary, what the Ten Commandments call for is nothing less than "the glorious freedom of the children of God" for which the whole creation groans and waits (cf. Romans 8:18-22). This is the classical structure of thought which the great Henri de Lubac rediscovered in our century and described as "the Christian paradox of the human creature": our created nature is from the very beginning oriented to a goal that exceeds its grasp, so that *sola gratia* is more than simply a response to sin.[27] There never was or could have been any thinkable fulfillment for our nature except in the generous grace of

27. Cf. Henri de Lubac, *The Mystery of the Supernatural,* trans. by Rosemary Sheed (New York: Herder & Herder, 1967).

God, embracing and drawing mortal dust into his fellowship — just as Israel could never be a kingdom of priests and a holy nation except under the LORD God's gracious dominion.

I think that it can be shown that Luther presupposes this traditional nature-grace paradigm, and that it underlies his theology of law and gospel.[28] If human beings are created to delight in God and serve God as the eye is made for vision or the voice for singing, then the will of God directing us to such love and service is never finally a mere exaction imposed externally on us. Our very existence is comprehended in the will of God articulated in the commandments; to turn from them is to turn against ourselves, to degrade ourselves, and in the end to destroy ourselves. If we do in fact experience the will of God as sheer crushing pressure from the outside, in the accusing law, it is because we have identified ourselves with our jailers and tormentors. As the Lutheran theologian Hans Joachim Iwand once wrote, "Precisely because the law is so good, and thinks so well of me, it makes my existence unbearable for me."[29] The law does not oppress us as an external limit on our freedom, and therefore an affront to our dignity; the commandments accuse us precisely by reminding us of the dignity for which God created us, and just so expose the degrading servitude into which we have fallen, and which we have embraced.

Thus for Luther, liberation means not only driving off the tyrants and jailers, but also the establishment of a true Lord and King in their place, Jesus Christ, who "rules over us by his righteousness, wisdom, power, life, and beatitude." That is, he rules over us by *giving himself* to us, for he is himself righteousness, wisdom, power, life, and beatitude, and just so he graciously accomplishes the will of the Father in us and among us. Our freedom therefore lies in *becoming his property*, as Luther provocatively puts it, coming under his sway, for only his gracious governance in the Spirit can free us for the dignity the Father designs for us. It is likewise for this reason that Luther views the ministry of the gospel not as the end of all governance, but as a distinctive sacramental *mode* of governance, through teaching and admonition, encouragement and warning, by which the gracious and patient but utterly serious *rule* of Christ the Lord is brought to bear on his people. It is in this light too that Luther can regard

---

28. I make a case for this in "Martin Luther on Law, Grace, and Moral Life: Prolegomena to an Ecumenical Discussion of *Veritatis Splendor*," forthcoming in *The Thomist.*

29. Hans Joachim Iwand, "Die Predigt des Gesetzes" in *Glaubensgerechtigkeit: Gesammelte Aufsätze II*, ed. by Gerhard Sauter (Munich: Christian Kaiser, 1980), p. 152.

not only the Key of absolution, but also the Key of binding, as an instrument of *gospel* ministry.

Already in Luther's own day, however, a different view of the self and its relation to God was coming on the scene. Where tradition saw the core of the self in its desire, its *amor,* its innate directedness towards the good,[30] emergent modernity began to identify the core of the self with "free will," now understood in a decidedly new way as a kind of monadic privacy, an ultimate detachment or disengagement prior to all engagements and relations.[31] And where traditional theology saw the dignity of the self precisely in the "upward call of God" (Philippians 3:14) to a *telos* beyond its scope, modernity came to locate the dignity of the self in its *power,* the power to impose its will on the world, or to realize its own authentic uniqueness despite the world, or to express itself in the raw material of the world.

Where the self is defined in terms of disengagement and power, the will of God comes to be seen as an external factor impinging on the self and limiting it from without. God's authority is reduced to his power to confer reward and impose punishment as we succeed or fail in meeting the exactions he imposes. The commandments of God are redefined as the articulation of these stipulations, and just so enter into an antithetical relationship to human freedom. Freedom easily comes to be defined as freedom precisely *from* the pressure of such demands, whether imposed by God or anyone else: we are free insofar as we can do what *we* want, insofar as our power is unchecked, unhindered by expectations or prohibitions imposed from outside ourselves.

All this, of course, is an impossibly broad-brush portrait of complex cultural and intellectual tendencies that have seldom, at least until recently, appeared in pure form. But it is nevertheless hard to deny that some such change in our underlying assumptions about the relation of self and God took place during the long transition to modernity. I want to point out very briefly two related ways in which this change has contributed to making the public exercise of the Keys unthinkable in mainline Protestantism today.

---

30. As Etienne Gilson put it, for the Augustinian tradition, "love is not something accidental and superadded, but a force within his [i.e. the human being's] essence, like the weight in a falling stone." Etienne Gilson, *The Christian Philosophy of Saint Augustine* (New York: Random House, 1960), p. 135.

31. On the development and character of modern notions of the self, cf. Charles Taylor, *Sources of the Self: The Making of the Modern Identity* (Cambridge, Mass.: Harvard University Press, 1989).

First of all, this new way of thinking about God and the self is surely somehow at the root of the remarkable obsession with *punishment* in early modern Christianity. Post-Reformation Protestants did not, of course, invent the notion of divine punishment, but never before had the whole problem of redemption been so single-mindedly defined in terms of escaping punishment. In the penal theories of atonement so prominent in early modern theology, the issue is not so much how Christ brings us to the Father's house as how Christ protects us from the Father's torments.[32] At the same time justification was separated from sanctification, and reduced to a pure verdict of acquittal declaring the sinner "off the hook" of eternal punishment. The sense of the forensic metaphor changed as the function of law changed in modern society: "acquittal" had once meant the restoration of honor and the reknitting of the bonds between the accused and the community, but in modern times it came increasingly to mean only a declaration that the state — or else God — would not, after all, impose penal sanctions on a particular individual.

The complete externalization of the divine-human relation was staved off for a time by recourse to the notion of guilt, another of modern Protestantism's obsessions. The issue between God and the self, it was said, is not only the punishment imposed by God upon the self, but the guilt recognized by both. The self was called to acknowledge the justice of God's condemnation, and to hear the echo of his accusation in its own sense of failure to live up to its best ideals. In retrospect, one suspects that this solution was always living on borrowed time; as the culture of modernity developed, guilt was inevitably exposed as only a more subtle imposition of punishment. In the demythologized faith of the middle classes — increasingly the only people mainline Protestant churches even tried to talk to — "guilt feelings" took the place once occupied by the pains of hell, and the question of redemption was reformulated from "How can we escape God's punishment?" to "How can we keep the concept of God from reinforcing our emotional pathologies?"

This brings us to a second point, which can be discussed quite briefly because it is so closely related to the first: the full impact on church discipline of modernity's reformulation of the divine-human relation was felt only as the modern self devolved from conqueror to victim. The crucial

---

32. Cf. the keen-sighted critique of this tendency in the work of the nineteenth-century Scottish theologian John MacLeod Campbell, *The Nature of the Atonement* (Grand Rapids: Eerdmans, reprint 1996).

turning-point here was surely Freud, though Freud should not be held responsible for the impudent bathos of our contemporary culture of victimhood. Freud's theory of the ego represents a sort of radicalization of the disengagement of the modern self; the ego is, as Charles Taylor puts it, "in essence a pure steering mechanism, devoid of instinctual force of its own. . . . Its job is to manoeuvre through the all-but-unnavigable obstacle course set by id, superego, and external reality."[33] Dissolve what might be called the Stoic element in Freud's thought, his stance of resigned unsentimentality, and it is an easy slide to regarding the self as a pure *coping*-mechanism, no longer "steering" with open-eyed resolve towards inevitable death, but quivering in place, scrambling desperately for mere survival against the voracious need of the id, the violent social cruelty internalized by the superego, and the indifferent brutality of the external world.

In the light of these changes, the first great gulf separating us from Luther comes fully into view: we no longer readily believe that it could be *good* news that we have a Lord and King. We cannot easily see how it would be a positive thing to fall under *any* definite governance with describable goals and substantive purposes, however gracious its operation. Since we no longer believe that human existence has any innate *telos* or end, except perhaps the purely formal and ungovernably pluralistic end of individual self-realization, the declaration that Christ will unfailingly accomplish the holy will of God in us, that his rule over us will assuredly secure our fulfillment of God's commandments, rings in our ears more like a threat than a promise. In the shadow of modern Protestantism's obsession with guilt and punishment, and the resentments bred thereby, and in this time when the once overtly aggressive modern self is declining into passive-aggressive victimhood, the very idea that there is a particular way God wants us to be appears as the great threat, the great burden, the cruelty that cannot be mitigated.

In such a climate, it is not only the public exercise of the Keys that becomes unthinkable; the central New Testament account of faith as acknowledgment of the authority of the crucified and risen Messiah, and hopeful submission to the wholesome discipline of his rule, has become alien to us. Our preachers hasten to assure us that God is "with us," that God is "there for us" in our struggles; but that divine presence mostly remains formless, a pure and therefore abstract affirmation which may

---

33. Charles Taylor, *Sources of the Self*, p. 174.

strengthen us for whatever is to come, but has no power to promise a future describably different from the present, a presence which therefore offers reassurance but not hope, the possibility of coping but not a new life. Indeed, we *identify* the graciousness of divine presence precisely with its lack of substantive purpose, its renunciation of dominion, its benign indifference to what we are and how we live. This is the chief historical peculiarity of contemporary mainline Christianity; never before in Christian history has the notion of salvation been so completely divorced from the notion of a hopeful discipline of life.

IV. Between Luther and Ourselves:
Christ and the World of Bodies

But this is not the only chasm separating us from Luther and the tradition in which he stood. Not only do we doubt that any divine governance could be gracious, we also doubt that Christ's governance in the Spirit could in any event hold sway in the world of bodies, that is, in the public world of concrete social interaction and exchange. Thus Luther's notion of the sanctification of the body, the corporate consecration of the Christian people in a distinctive mode of public presence, a distinctive way of life, marks another difference that demands our attention.

Recent studies have suggested how crucial a particular notion of "religion" was to the whole rise of modern culture and indeed of the modern state.[34] This modern notion of religion was from the start a device for removing Christianity and its dangerous claims about God's dominion from the public realm, and confining their direct implications to an inner sphere of personal spirituality, the inner world of the disengaged self. Public truth about the real world would henceforth be *secular* truth, quarried from phenomena by the methods of natural and social science; religion could affect the attitude of the inner person to the "facts" thus discovered, but could never make public claims about what is the case — potentially at odds with the consensus of experts. Therefore the possibilities for public action would likewise be defined by the "facts" known to social science; re-

---

34. Cf. especially John Milbank, *Theology and Social Theory* (Oxford: Blackwell, 1990). I have examined the effects of this on mainline Christianity more extensively in "Messiah's People: The Culture of the Church in the Midst of the Nations," *Pro Ecclesia* 6 (1997): 146-71.

ligion might provide us with inward motivation as we consider our options, but could not give distinctive public form to social life.

Luther's talk of "two kingdoms" has been pressed into service to give theological legitimacy to this modern internalization of religion, but in fact the whole scheme is alien to him. For Luther, God's justifying act sanctifies the bodies of his people, gathers and forms them to a distinctive mode of public presence in the world. This is coherent with Luther's insistence that faith itself has a bodily, public dimension: faith is not something that can occur merely in the private space between a person's two ears; it is bodily involvement with a bodily world, with the gospel and sacraments proclaimed and celebrated out in public in the assembly of the church. Therefore Luther's faith, however much it involves the heart, is nonetheless from the start a mode of public behavior, a public positioning of the body. To believe is to find oneself bound bodily by the gospel to the bodily communion of the Christian people,[35] to find oneself caught up in the distinctive common life formed by the seven holy things of which Luther writes in *On the Councils:* the proclaimed word, baptism, the Supper, the discipline of the Keys, the governance of the gospel ministry, the liturgy of prayer, praise, and thanksgiving, and the bearing of the holy cross. These are the means by which the Spirit sanctifies not only the soul but also the body, shaping our bodily life in all its dimensions in anticipation of the life of the coming age.

Thus for Luther, talk of "two kingdoms" does not mark a distinction between the public and the private, between the bodily world and the inner secrecy of the heart. On the contrary, such talk identifies two *public* modes of governance, each outward and bodily, the sword on the left hand and the word on the right, each founding a distinct sort of public space, the polity and the church. Between these two, and somehow underlying them, is the third "estate" founded by God, the household, likewise a kind of public social space. The relations between these three public estates are complex; Luther may tend in some moods to over-harmonize them, but he never denies that Christ exercises a public and bodily dominion in the

---

35. The relationship between faith and entry into the Christian community is precisely stated in the *Large Catechism:* "I believe that there is a holy little congregation and assembly on the earth made up of pure saints under one head, Christ, called together by the Holy Spirit, in one faith, mind, and understanding, with manifold gifts, yet harmonious in love, without sects and schism. I am also a part and member of this assembly, brought in and incorporated by the Holy Spirit, by virtue of having heard and still hearing God's word, which is the beginning of entry into this community." *BSELK,* p. 657.

church: "You can see, therefore, how the dominion of this King works. In His invisible essence, He sits at the right hand of God; but He rules visibly on earth and works through external, visible signs, of which the preaching of the Gospel and the Sacraments are the chief ones, and through public confession and the fruits of faith in the Gospel."[36]

Moreover, not only does Luther deny the modern equation of religion with private inwardness, he also denies the other pillar of modern secularism, the identification of the "real" world with the secular world. The polity and the household are, to be sure, "secular" estates, governed by "reason," but only in the sense that they are concerned with affairs of this present; the "world," that is, the total context, in which they operate, and with which "reason" reckons, on the other hand, is by no means "secular," but rather theologically and scripturally defined. Indeed, the church's chief obligation to the other estates is to tell them the truth about the world and thus about themselves. Luther makes room for a relative independence of secular learning, but only faith knows where the world comes from, by whom it is ruled, and to what end. In contemporary jargon, only faith knows what "narrative" embraces and orders reason's bits and pieces of this-worldly knowledge. Thus for Luther, the resurrection and exaltation of Christ are public truths, with political significance; prayer is a significant form of political action, with whose efficacy wise rulers will reckon; and the doctrine of the angels is part of political science, essential to an accurate description of the way things go in public life.[37]

---

36. *Exposition of Psalm 110, On the Kingdom and Glory of Christ*, WA 41; LW 13:272.

37. On the political relevance of the resurrection and exaltation, cf. Luther's sermons on 1 Corinthians 15 (1532-1533), *WA* 36, *LW* 28:123-31. On prayer as political power, cf. the *Exposition of the Gospel According to St. John 14–16* (1537), *WA* 45:534-37; *LW* 24:80-84: "But we, as Christians, must know that the whole system of earthly government stands and remains for its allotted time solely through God's order and command and the prayers of Christians" (81). For a sample of Luther's political angelology, cf. the first sermon for St. Michael and All Angels in Eugene F. A. Klug, ed., *Sermons of Martin Luther: The House Postils*, vol. 3 (Grand Rapids: Baker, 1996), pp. 378-79: "If, therefore, the beloved angels were not at the courts of the emperor, kings, and princes, the devil would be in control; it is evident that no harmony can be created there, for the devil whispers things into their ears and causes all manner of dissensions. And were the dear angels not there to prevent these things from happening, they would tear into one another all the time and not a day would pass without war and bloodshed. Our Lord God allows noble lords to be at loggerheads; at times he allows the devil to light a fire, but then you will find the beloved angels extinguishing the fire and making peace. However, where God pulls back his angels because of our sins, there people flare up, murder, kill, and violate women, to the great delight of the devil."

Therefore, though Luther knows that the bodily sanctification of the Christian people is hindered and opposed in many ways by the world, the flesh, and the devil, it would never occur to him that the struggle for corporate holiness could founder on "facts," on the resistance of an autonomous "secular" reality impervious to spiritual governance. And this, I would suggest, brings us to the brink of another great gulf separating Luther from contemporary mainline Protestantism, for the moral history of the Protestant mainline in the last two centuries has been a long retreat from one arena of bodily life after another, a series of withdrawals from the project of corporeal sanctification into the inward realm of attitude and feeling and disposition. This retreat has been masked by a great deal of storm and bluster over issues in public life; but the theme of these disputes has tended more and more to be how inward Christian attitudes should dispose us to choose amongst alternatives formed and defined by secular processes. The notion that God's justifying act through the gospel might itself shape and define public reality, that the Christian people *gathered* by that act might also be *formed* by it in a corporeally concrete mode of life, scarcely even makes an appearance in our denominational controversies.

In this light, the revisions of sexual morality proposed in nearly every mainline denomination during this decade seem less an aberration than a natural continuation of modern Protestant history. After all, in mainline churches we no longer expect that the Christian household will be a distinctive sort of economic unit, or that Christian parents will encourage their children to pursue certain kinds of employment and avoid others, or that Christian congregations will do anything but mirror the racial divisions in the surrounding society, or that there will be serious scrutiny in the churches of the justice of particular wars and ways of making war, with binding consequences for the faithful, or that Christian couples will be accountable to the ecclesial community for their fidelity to their marriage vows. These realms of life have all been declared outside the competence of the church, subject to laws and forces defined by secular social science, and thus not amenable to the sanctifying governance of the Spirit. So when it is argued today that with whom and under what conditions we couple is determined by the autonomous pressure of something called "human sexuality," with which the church should not try to meddle, the development is not surprising nor the mode of argument novel. Indeed, today's "liberal" sexual revisionists sound like nothing so much as "conservative" apologists for militarism in Wilhelmine Germany; the underlying assumptions and the structure of the arguments are identical.

Again and again during the last two centuries, mainline Protestantism has retreated from bodily life under the pressure of a three-stranded argument. It has been argued, first, that the church *cannot* give any distinctive form to these realms of life or to the participation of Christians therein; economic life, war, race relations, marriage and divorce, and human sexuality generally have all at different times been declared realms of ineluctable fact, governed by autonomous laws and trends and probabilities, in the face of which any effort on the part of the church to exercise a formative governance in the name of Christ would only invite ridicule. In the second place, moreover, it has been argued that the church *should not* attempt to interfere with these realms of life or to live distinctively within them; the church's proper ministry is to the inner life, to the realm of feeling and attitude and motivation, and it demeans the church to abandon that sublime sphere to meddle with the shape of things in the bodily world. Finally, it is urged that it would be *cruel* to seek a distinctive formation of the life of the Christian people in these realms; the outcome of the attempt could only be to encourage self-righteousness in those who conform easily to superficial legality, while loading intolerable guilt upon others caught up in social and historical processes over which they have no control.

The upshot of this long history of retreat is a deep-seated assumption in mainline churches that the mission of the gospel reaches its goal in the private consciousness of the individual, in the inner experience of acceptance or wholeness or affirmation or the like. Nothing is expected to happen out in public when the gospel is preached; the lordship of Christ asserted therein is not understood to claim any space for itself in the bodily world. Here again, it is not only the public exercise of the Keys that becomes unthinkable in such a climate. What has most fundamentally become alien to us is the central New Testament conception of the church, the renewed people of God at the end of days, gathered together by God's justifying act to be a sign to the nations and a light to the world. To grant the distinctive peoplehood of the church sufficient social density that it could be *seen* by the nations is just what mainline Protestants have come to regard as at best in poor taste, and at worst heartlessly authoritarian.

V. Conclusion: Faithfulness in a Day of Small Things

There is no honest way of avoiding the conclusion: by Luther's standards — and here he speaks for a wide ecumenical tradition — our mainline churches today are churches in trouble. The disappearance of corporate discipline is more than the abandonment of ancient custom now grown uncouth; it marks the point at which a whole array of fears and confusions and wayward cultural codes conspire to alienate us from the faith and the mission of the apostolic church. This alienation is deep enough that it must seriously call into question the capacity of mainline churches, as presently constituted, to represent the reign of the crucified and risen Christ before the world. Nor is there any prospect of immediate reform. God can always surprise us, but humanly speaking, it seems profoundly improbable that mainline churches will recover in our lifetimes the sort of vigorous public exercise of the Keys that Luther envisioned.

If any of us are to continue, in the face of these uncomfortable realities, to regard mainline churches as authentic arenas of Christian ministry, it can only be because, as George Lindbeck has written, "The identity of the chosen people in the new age as in the old depends utterly on God's election, not on its own faithfulness or unfaithfulness."[38] That is to say, our communities have received God's irrevocable gifts and calling in Holy Baptism (cf. Romans 11:29), and therefore we may hear as a word to ourselves the declaration of the prophet Zechariah (8:6-8):

> Thus says the Lord of hosts: Even though it seems impossible to the remnant of this people in these days, should it also seem impossible to me, says the Lord of hosts? Thus says the Lord of hosts: I will save my people from the east country and from the west country; and I will bring them to live in Jerusalem. They shall be my people and I will be their God, in faithfulness and in righteousness.

Such words grant us no bland assurance that our *status quo* is really all right after all; they promise rather that God will give our communities no rest until they have been brought, through presently unimaginable judgments and tribulations, into some future reconfiguration of the holy catholic church. They call us in the meantime neither to barren impatience nor to dull conformity but to faithfulness in what the prophet calls "the day of small things" (Zechariah 4:10), a day when seemingly nothing great or significant can be done, in comparison with our danger, a day when only little steps can be taken, easy to despise, yet which the Lord will not let be in vain.

38. George A. Lindbeck, "The Story-Shaped Church: Critical Exegesis and Theological Interpretation" in Garrett Green, ed., *Scriptural Authority and Narrative Interpretation* (Minneapolis: Fortress, 1987), pp. 161-78, here p. 167.

In conclusion, therefore, I want very briefly to point out four areas in which recent developments may be making "small things" possible in mainline churches, little steps which may seem insignificant but nonetheless open out towards a future in which the exercise of the Keys, and with it the very idea of a corporate discipline of life, will no longer seem unthinkable among us. I do not suggest that these developments are *unambiguously* positive or promising, only that they represent junctures of opportunity which hard pastoral labor might turn to good account.

The first such juncture is the untidy bundle of disparate concerns and interests to which we typically refer these days as "spirituality." Undoubtedly much of what passes under that title is part of the problem rather than any potential element in the solution, religious consumer goods for the disengaged self in this time of its decadence.[39] Yet it would be a mistake to assume that the contemporary fascination for spirituality constitutes any *single* movement or phenomenon; it is rather a kind of thick soup composed of divergent and even contradictory desires and motivations, often existing simultaneously inside the same heads. Experience and observation have convinced me that *one* ingredient in that soup is a groping after something mainline Christianity has largely lost, a hopeful discipline of life through which Christ's gracious governance might begin to give form and direction to our lives. It guarantees no long-term outcome, but neither is it entirely insignificant, that terms like "formation" and "direction" have reentered our vocabulary in a positive sense. At the very least, it provides an opportunity to open up in a concrete way in our churches questions about faith and discipleship, God's grace and Christ's reign, and about the formative role of the church itself as a community of common practice, mutual upbuilding and exhortation — and perhaps even mutual accountability.

As a second juncture of opportunity, I would point to contemporary concerns about violence towards women and children, which have given rise to complaints from unlikely quarters about the moral *laissez-faire* in mainline churches. Here again, I do not underestimate the ambiguity of the phenomena, the tangled politics of domestic violence and abuse in the culture at large as well as in the churches. But at the very least it can be said that this movement of concern has intruded into mainline Protestant dis-

---

39. On this, cf. L. Gregory Jones's splendid evisceration of the "consumer spirituality" of contemporary guru Thomas Moore: "A Thirst for God or Consumer Spirituality? Cultivating Disciplined Practices of Being Engaged by God," *Modern Theology* 13 (1997): 3-28.

course a category long absent from it: the category of the *intolerable*. Nor is violence towards the vulnerable an obviously bad place to begin reflecting on what might constitute intolerable behavior in the Christian community; a case can be made, apart from all ideology, that questions about power and violence have a *constitutional* centrality in the common life of the Christian people. The gospel is, after all, a message whose central theme is power and authority, the peculiar engagement of God's power in the crucified Lord Jesus to inaugurate his kingdom. Thus when the church finds it tolerable that the strong in its midst abuse the weak, it denies the lordship which it exists to represent in a quite singular way.

But what would it mean practically for our churches to recognize that there is indeed such a thing as behavior which they cannot tolerate? What would be required institutionally for them to take action on such recognition, without rushing headlong into a whole new series of abuses? Such questions open onto others: What would it mean to understand the church as more than an association for the promotion of piety, or a religious service-provider on the open market, or a counselling center with intermittent worship services? What would it mean to understand the church as an authentic *polity*, a community in which a real though gracious *governance* is exercised, *sine human vi sed verbo,* "without human coercion but by the word" (*Augsburg Confession* XXVIII)? Here again, no smooth way opens for us into the future, only a starting point for wrestling concretely with questions to which we now assuredly have no clear answers.[40]

As a third juncture of opportunity, I would point to what appears to be a shift occurring in the wider cultural consensus regarding divorce. This shift has so far made scarcely a ripple in the corporate life of mainline churches; according to Barbara Dafoe Whitehead, secular psychotherapists seem far more concerned about marriage and its health than mainline Protestant clergy.[41] The reasons for this are undoubtedly deep-seated: the latter-day Protestant suspicion that form and order equal cruelty finds perhaps its most sacrosanct and intensely guarded expression in the main-

40. One of the best introductions to this complex of concerns, especially with reference to the Office of the Keys, is the brief but wise essay of Sharon Zanter Ross, "A Pastoral Response to Incest," *Lutheran Forum* (Pentecost, 1987): 12-15.

41. Cf. Whitehead's contribution to the symposium "End No-Fault Divorce?" *First Things* 75 (August/September): 27-30, here 29. See also Whitehead, *The Divorce Culture* (New York: Knopf, 1997). Whatever the ultimate adequacy of Whitehead's position, her book should be required as Lenten reading for mainline Protestant clergy.

line culture of divorce. But that only makes this opportunity, slender though it is, all the more significant, for even the slightest crack in the divorce culture would, I am convinced, shake the overall moral and theological culture of our denominations to its core.

The starting point, however, cannot be the bare *imposition* of responsibility on married couples as private persons, or indeed the imposition of guilt on the already divorced, but rather the corporate *assumption* of responsibility for marriage by the ecclesial community, led by its pastors. We need to begin by asking, "What difference does membership in the church make to one's expectations of marriage, to one's ethic of marriage, and to the environment of one's marriage?" This is central to the Reformer's insight into marriage: accountability for marriage does not begin or end with the responsibility of each married couple, though that certainly cannot be denied. Rather, the church itself, as a community, along with its ministry, is accountable to God for marriage and the formation of marriage. The church is called to be a distinctive environment for marriage, where men and women are taught to see and interpret married life as an arena for discipleship, for witness together to the dominion of Christ the Lord.[42] The church's responsibility for marriage is thus inseparable from the church's central commission to represent in the midst of the nations the governance of Christ by which the will of the Father — his design "from the beginning of creation" (Mark 10:6) — is graciously accomplished. Only by grasping the issue of marriage and divorce as a question first of all about the church's mission will we be addressing the issues that genuinely threaten us.

The fourth and final opportunity is the most significant of all, for it offers the indispensable framework within which alone the others can bear ultimate fruit. I refer to the remarkable phenomenon of moves, within mainline denominations, towards the institution of an adult catechumenate, modelled more or less closely on the Roman Catholic *Rite for the Christian Initiation of Adults.* Here too the opportunity is fragile: the pro-

---

42. As Luther put it in the *Fastenpostille* of 1525, "Everything that is God's word and work, if it is to be blessed at all, must proceed in such a way that it is sour, bitter, and grievous to the outer person. Therefore marriage too is an estate which promotes and provides practice in faith in God and love for neighbor through manifold struggles, labors, annoyances, crosses, and every sort of unpleasantness . . ." *WA* 17/2:62; cf. Lenker, vol. 2, p. 56. What would be required to put that vision, rather than our culture's assumption that marriage is an entitlement to emotional and sexual satisfaction, at the heart of what people learn about marriage by living in the church?

grams to which I refer have no great supporting constituency in the churches, and what they envision would require labor-intensive commitment from both pastors and people. Yet here too the fragility of the opening is in direct proportion to its importance; the adult catechumenate seems like a hard sell in mainline churches precisely because it runs counter to so many of their deepest and most damaging assumptions. Indeed, I would suggest that the development of a liturgically structured adult catechumenate, embedded in the life of the congregation and involving a wide range of its members, is among the most profoundly subversive projects possible in a mainline denomination today.

By its very structure, the catechumenate sets forth the church as a community with a distinct mode of life into which an initiation is needed, an alternative society whose peculiar ways need to be investigated by inquirers and adapted to by newcomers. The catechumenate thus presents baptism as reception into a community of *disciples,* called to distinctive life and witness. By this very stroke, salvation itself is interpreted as something other than contentless divine acceptance; it means coming under the rule of Jesus, sharing in the life and mission of his people. Finally, there is a deep connection between the structure of the catechumenate and the classical Christian understanding of human persons, for the catechumenal process invites those who take part in it to find their own destiny figured in Israel's journey to the promised land; it describes them to themselves as wayfarers seeking a goal they can only attain by submitting to the Lord's gracious governance.[43]

Here again I do not suggest that the adult catechumenate is a quick fix for all that ails us; but it is among the most significant steps available to us by which we can build for a different future. A congregation whose perceptions of Christian community and Christian faith had been shaped for several generations by the year-in, year-out practice of the adult catechumenate might well find itself ready to entertain thoughts now unthinkable in mainline churches; and on that readiness the future of our churches as recognizably *Christian* communities will almost certainly depend.

43. Marva Dawn briefly and gracefully works out the connections between an Augustinian anthropology, the understanding of the church as "alternative society," and the catechumenate in her essay, "How Does Contemporary Culture Yearn for God?" in *Welcome to Christ: A Lutheran Introduction to the Catechumenate* (Minneapolis: Augsburg Fortress, 1997), pp. 35-47. Cf. also Pamela E. J. Jackson, *Journeybread for the Shadowlands: The Readings for the Rites of the Catechumenate, RCIA* (Collegeville, Minn.: Liturgical Press, 1993).

ORDINATION

The Special Ministry of the Ordained

CARL E. BRAATEN

Introduction

In his treatise "On the Councils and the Church" Martin Luther called the ordained ministry the fifth distinguishing mark of the church, after discussing the preaching of the Word, the sacrament of baptism, the Lord's Supper, and the power of the keys. He wrote: "The church is recognized externally by the fact that it consecrates or calls ministers, or has offices that it is to administer. There must be bishops, pastors, or preachers, who publicly and privately give, administer, and use the aforementioned things or holy possessions in behalf of and in the name of the church, or rather by reason of their institution by Christ. . . . Now wherever you find these offices or officers, you may be assured that the holy Christian people are there; for the church cannot be without these bishops, pastors, preachers, priests, and conversely, they cannot be without the church. Both must be together."[1]

To call the ordained ministry a mark of the church means that it is essential; the church cannot exist without it. The ecumenical dialogues have demonstrated broad consensus on this point. And yet this mark of the church — or some facet pertaining to it — is the one most hotly disputed within our churches and between the churches.

The scope of this chapter will be limited mostly to problems of the special ministry, ordination, and succession within the Lutheran tradition.

---

1. Martin Luther, "On the Councils and the Church," *Luther's Works*, vol. 41 (Philadelphia: Fortress Press, 1966), pp. 154, 164.

Conrad Bergendoff once wrote: "In no area of doctrine has the Lutheran church in America had greater difficulty than in the matter of the ministry."[2] We could update that remark and say: "In no area has the Evangelical Lutheran Church in America had greater difficulty than in the matter of ministry." Trouble started before it was born, conceived in the womb of the Commission for a New Lutheran Church (CNLC). Edgar R. Trexler opened his account of its proceedings in *Anatomy of a Merger,* saying: "No one ever tried to put a church together the way the Lutheran Church in America (LCA), the American Lutheran Church (ALC), and the Association of Evangelical Lutheran Churches (AELC) did in the mid-1980s."[3]

The Commission (CNLC) could reach no agreement on the ordering of ministry. The strangest opinions were voiced. A prominent LCA bishop said: "We want to recognize the episcopal character of oversight that repudiates apostolic succession in principle. Apostolic succession is a perversion of the historic episcopate."[4] The presiding bishop of the ALC, speaking in favor of increasing lay representation at assemblies, said: "The clergy are not representative of the mind of the church."[5] Speaking for the ALC one theologian said that that church body tends more toward the transference theory,[6] a view coming from the low-church tradition "whose rationale for the office of ordained ministry was that their authority was derived from the congregation delegating it to pastors."[7] In fact the Constitution of the ALC declared that "the status of the clergy differs from that of the laity *only as to function.*"[8] Here the doctrine of the ministry, qualified by its distinctive component elements of ordination and succession, is reduced to pure functionalism. Trexler summed it up: "Since Lutherans in America had never agreed on a doctrine of the ministry, it may have been unrealistic to think that a consensus was possible given the different views within the CNLC — some 'high' clerical views, some 'populist' thinking, and the AELC's unilateral expansion to include teachers as part of the office of ministry."[9]

2. Conrad Bergendoff, *The Doctrine of the Church in American Lutheranism,* p. 19.

3. Edgar R. Trexler, *Anatomy of a Merger* (Minneapolis: Augsburg, 1991), ix.

4. *Anatomy of a Merger,* p. 66.

5. *Anatomy of a Merger,* p. 99.

6. *Anatomy of a Merger,* p. 117.

7. *Anatomy of a Merger,* p. 65.

8. *The Constitution and Bylaws of the American Lutheran Church,* edition of 1987, 6.32-33, p. 59. (Italics mine)

9. *Anatomy of a Merger,* pp. 142-43.

What a way to organize a new church body, without basic agreement on the doctrine of the ministry! Could this possibly mean that the status of the doctrine itself had been devalued to that of an *adiaphoron*, something Lutherans are ready to treat as a matter of theological indifference in the name of Christian freedom? The upshot was that the Commission passed the ball to the future, placing the unresolved problems in the hands of a Task Force of 17 persons appointed to study the ministry for five years at the cost of more than a million dollars. (Actually a budget was adopted with the cumulative total of $1,338,000.) I was one of the 17 selected on the basis of the quota system the CNLC had stipulated for the new church body. This experience did not make me a believer in quotas. For it meant that theology would be treated as one category, subordinate to the distinctions of gender, color, clergy, and laity. One of this, one of that, one of these, and one of those — one New Testament and one dogmatic theologian, one bishop and one seminary president, but no Old Testament theologian and no church historians from the ancient and medieval periods.

The Task Force was given a daunting assignment: to articulate "a Lutheran understanding and adaptation of the threefold ministerial office of bishop, pastor, and deacon and its ecumenical implication," and it was mandated to do this on the basis of "sound doctrinal principles relating to ministry as presented by biblical and confessional norms, and as informed by church history developments."

This was potentially a kairotic moment in American Lutheranism. For now we could take advantage of the leverage of the ecumenical dialogues and the challenge of the Faith and Order statement on *Baptism, Eucharist, and Ministry* (BEM) to end the Lutheran legacy of ambiguity on ministry and reconnect with the Great Tradition which for tragic reasons was disrupted by the schism of the sixteenth century. Once the membership and leadership of the Task Force were announced, failure was easily and widely predicted. The designated chairman, John Reumann, had already published his views on episcopacy and the threefold office of ministry.[10] He stated: "Lutherans remain free to adopt the title bishop, especially if they are clear what a Lutheran concept of episcopacy excludes, namely, lifelong tenure of office and title, new power in placing clergy not now given to synodical presidents, hierarchical status, ontological change, apostolic succession in the sense of transmission of grace by office from a chain of predecessors, or a threefold ministry and his-

10. John H. P. Reumann, *Ministries Examined* (Minneapolis: Augsburg, 1987).

125

toric episcopate."[11] This would be news to the Churches of Sweden and Finland — that the historic episcopate is contrary to their Lutheran understanding of ministry. And what's the point of adopting the title bishop if virtually everything traditionally associated with the office is excluded? If American Lutheran bishops are exactly like all other pastors, only with a different job description, then why do so many, from the day of installation into office, wear purple rabats and pectoral crosses? Are these symbols without substance?

We are frankly indulging in a bit of typical Lutheran in-fighting. But this topic inescapably invites polemics. My thesis is threefold: first, that Lutherans have been and are still confused on the doctrine of the ministry; second, that there is no way to resolve the difficulty by going more deeply into our own confessional sources because they bear the imprint of ambiguity inherent in Luther's own statements on ministry; and third, and most importantly, there is no ecumenically viable way out of this morass without eventually realigning and reconciling Lutheran ordained ministry with the episcopally ordained ministries in apostolic succession in the Eastern and Western branches of the one holy catholic church. I believe this is a realistic assessment and not mere wishful thinking. The alternative is to remain in our separated ecclesial enclaves, resulting in the abortion of the ecumenical movement. For the aim of the ecumenical movement is not getting Christians to be nice to each other; its goal is a universal communion (koinonia) of churches joined together in the one apostolic faith and the one body of Christ.

I. A Legacy of Ambiguity

Every generation of Lutherans has looked to Luther and the Confessions for clear answers to questions that keep backing up like bad plumbing. (1) Is the office of ministry divinely instituted or does it originate in the need of a congregation for good order? (2) How does it come about, through a transference of the rights and powers that belong to all believers and delegated to one minister, or through a transmission of gifts by ministers already in office? (3) Does ordination possess sacramental character, by which the Holy Spirit bestows a charism through prayer and the laying on of hands, or is it essentially a ceremony of installation and ratification

---

11. *Ministries Examined*, p. 154.

of a congregational call? (4) What sorts of ministerial acts may lay persons perform and under what conditions? Can they preach, baptize, administer communion, lead worship, absolve, ordain, and teach?

Lutherans have traditionally held that in cases of emergency lay persons may baptize but not administer communion; they have allowed lay persons to preach — always a dangerous thing — but not to ordain. But why not? If the transference theory were correct, it would be more consistent to have ordination performed by lay leaders of the congregation. For Luther said: "When a bishop consecrates it is nothing else than that in the place and stead of the whole community, all of whom have like power, he takes a person and charges him to exercise this power on behalf of the others. It is like ten brothers, all king's sons and equal heirs, choosing one of themselves to rule the inheritance in the interest of all. In one sense they are all kings and of equal power, and yet one of them is charged with the responsibility of ruling. To put it still more clearly: suppose a group of earnest Christian laymen were taken prisoner and set down in a desert without an episcopally ordained priest among them. And suppose they were to come to a common mind there and then in the desert and elect one of their number, whether he were married or not, and charge him to baptize, say mass, pronounce absolution, and preach the gospel. Such a man would be as truly a priest as though he had been ordained by all the bishops and popes in the world. That is why in cases of necessity anyone can baptize and give absolution. This would be impossible if we were not all priests."[12] This is the favorite passage of those who hold the theory of transference, the so-called *"Übertragungslehre."* A long line of Lutheran theologians have ridden this rail, appealing to Luther — J. W. F. Hoefling (1802-1853), G. C. A. von Harless (1806-1879), Gottfried Thomasius (1802-1875), C. F. W. Walther (1811-1887), Georg Sverdrup (1848-1907), Matthias Loy (1820-1915), and more recently Wilhelm Brunotte, Ernst Käsemann, Herman Diem, Wilhelm Joest, Gustaf Wingren, and Per Erik Persson, to mention only a few.

G. H. Gerberding in his classic, *The Lutheran Pastor,* written at the beginning of this century, called attention to the legacy of ambiguity that Luther left the movement named after him on the doctrine of the ministry. He quoted the opinions of a number of Luther-scholars at the time. J. P. Mueller says: "Luther's expressions concerning the office of the ministry are uncertain. . . . He can make no clear distinction between the office of

12. *Luther's Works,* vol. 44, p. 128.

the ministry and the universal priesthood."[13] H. E. Jacobs says that Luther's language is "not guarded with the same care as that of the later dogmaticians."[14]

Critics of the transference theory, however, find quite another line of thinking in Luther. Luther wrote, for example: "According to the institution of Christ and the apostles, every city should have a priest or bishop."[15] Many passages can be cited where Luther firmly insisted that the office of ministry was mandated by God. So the institution theory also has a long lineage in Lutheranism — August Vilmar, Friedrich Julius Stahl, Wilhelm Löhe, Wilhelm Stählin, Friedrich Heiler, Nathan Söderblom, Regin Prenter, Edmund Schlink, and Arthur Carl Piepkorn, to pick a few representatives from various countries.

What's going on when theologians from the same tradition can appeal to the same sources — Luther and the Confessions — and come up with opposing answers to the fundamental questions about the office of ministry, ordination, and apostolic succession? Far from being a harmless dispute among "ivory tower" theologians, this basic disagreement was apparent in the Commission for a New Lutheran Church, in the Task Force for the Study of Ministry, and at the ELCA 1997 assembly in Philadelphia at which the laity had the majority of votes.

II. Exegetical and Dogmatic Dissensus

The Task Force was mandated to apply biblical and confessional norms to its study and recommendations on ministry. This is what Lutherans usually do — go to the Scriptures (the *norma normans*) and interpret them in light of the Creeds and Confessions (the *norma normata*). So what happened? Everywhere we looked we were greeted by the same legacy of ambiguity.[16] The opinions of the biblical experts ride the same divergent rails

13. G. H. Gerberding, *The Lutheran Pastor* (Philadelphia: Lutheran Publication Society, 1902), pp. 74, 75.

14. *The Lutheran Pastor*, pp. 74, 75.

15. M. Luther, "To the Christian Nobility," *Luther's Works*, vol. 44, p. 175.

16. Todd Nichol has correctly observed that "from the late 1960s to the present there has been steadily increasing tension among American Lutherans over the doctrine of the ministry. As it has taken shape, the debate over ministry has often engendered a polemical spirit and the argument has from time to time descended from its original sophistication to caricature and canard." "Ministry and Oversight in American Lutheranism," *Called and Or-*

on ministry. The Task Force invited two prominent American New Testament scholars to lecture on ministry in the early church, Roy A. Harrisville and Karl Donfried. Harrisville represented a line of New Testament interpretation[17] that included Hans F. von Campenhausen, Eduard Schweizer, and especially Ernst Käsemann.

For Ernst Käsemann the ambiguity on ministry exists already in the New Testament. Paul believed that all Christians are endowed by the Spirit with charisms, all the baptized are office-bearers responsible for carrying out the ministry of the word of God, and none are specially commissioned with the prerogative of official proclamation over against the rest of the community. But in the generation after Paul a transition took place, the first fall of the church, as it were, into what Käsemann calls "early catholicism," appearing in full bloom in the Pastoral Epistles. A radical change took place from a charismatic concept of ministry to an institutional ordering of ministry.

Käsemann describes the change this way: "The apostolic delegate is regarded in the Pastorals as the connecting link between apostle and monarchial bishop. . . . His work is to continue the apostolic office in the subapostolic age. In other words, he stands in the apostolic succession . . . in virtue of the Spirit imparted to him through ordination. This is the genesis of that conception of ministerial office which is to determine the course of events hereafter. The distinction between clerics and laymen is now in *being,* in practice if not in theory. It is now tacitly accepted that the authority of the institutional ministry is guaranteed by a principle of tradition and legitimate succession which has become the basis of all Church order; and this (episcopal) ministry has surrounded itself with various executive organs in the shape of the presbyterate, the diaconate and the order of widows. . . . This shows that the Pauline conception of a Church order based on charisma disappeared in the very church the Apostle himself created."[18]

Käsemann asks: "How did this come about?"[19] His answer: "The weight of the gnostic attack threatened to overwhelm the Christian community. . . . The method chosen was, first, to entrust teaching and adminis-

---

dained, ed. by Todd Nichol and Marc Kolden (Minneapolis: Fortress Press, 1990), p. 107. Nichol, of course, does more than his share to contribute to this "descent."

17. Cf. Roy A. Harrisville, *Ministry in Crisis* (Minneapolis: Augsburg, 1987).

18. Ernst Käsemann, "Ministry and Community in the New Testament," *Essays on New Testament Themes* (London: SCM Press, 1964), p. 88.

19. "Ministry and Community," p. 88.

tration to reliable hands and to create a settled ministry against which alien pretensions would beat in vain; then to tie this ministry to a solemn ordination vow (and thus to rule out unsuitable elements) and to surround it with auxiliaries bound by similar obligations, thus guaranteeing the care of the whole community down to the most insignificant members; and finally to insert the ministry into a fabricated chain of tradition and to render its position impregnable by a doctrine of legitimate succession."[20]

Harrisville and Donfried did not actually enter into a debate face to face. Their irreconcilable views were simply presented side by side. Donfried rather directed his attack at Käsemann. Käsemann's depiction of the rise of early catholic developments in the Pastoral Epistles, he acknowleged, is mostly to be accepted, though Käsemann exaggerates the difference between the Pauline and the Pastoral Letters. What is unacceptable is Käsemann's denial of the apostolic legitimacy of this development based on the principle that a *"theologia gloriae* is now in process of replacing the *theologia crucis."*[21]

Donfried observed that "at the root of Käsemann's critique is a canon within the canon that is so narrow and restrictive that it excludes whatever is not representative of his understanding of Paul. According to this same critierion . . . the collection of Paul's letters, the formation of the canon, the historic creeds and the ordained ministry themselves are all examples of a *theologia gloriae.* To follow Käsemann's position to its logical conclusion would lead the church into an enthusiastic sectarianism, and that, of course, was the very battle the church had to fight over against gnosticism in its early history."[22] Among those whose views Donfried adduced to support his arguments are Harold Riesenfeld, H. D. Wendland, Jerome D. Quinn, Raymond Brown, Brevard Childs, and Leonard Goppelt.

In moving from the exegetical to the dogmatic level the legacy of ambiguity remained intact. The Task Force was confronted by opposing hermeneutics of the Christian tradition, and especially of the Reformation. The chief texts that came into play for consideration were the sixteenth-century Confessional Writings (of Luther and Melanchthon) and the twentieth-century ecumenical dialogues. Here two opposing sides glared at each other across the line of scrimmage, one seeing Lutheran-

---

20. "Ministry and Community," p. 88.
21. "Ministry and Community," p. 92.
22. Karl Donfried, "Ministry and the New Testament," p. 16. (Unpublished paper.)

ism as an evangelical catholic movement, the other in terms of denominational Protestantism.

The evangelical catholic reading of the Confessions sees the office of ministry as a constitutive public mark of the church, one based not on the universal priesthood but on Christ and his apostles. Ordination is an essential requirement with sacramental character, as the Apology of the Augsburg Confession affirms (Article 13); it bestows a charism, that is, spiritual authority to represent Christ and the gospel over against the congregation. The ministerial office assumed its classical threefold structuring of bishop, presbyter, and deacon very early on, before the formation of the New Testament canon and the Apostles' Creed.

An element of the Catholic idea of *"character indelebilis"* is affirmed in the Lutheran practice of ordaining for life and thus only once. Only those who are ordained may ordain, and according to Article 14 of the *Apology of the Augsburg Confession* Lutherans confess their "deep desire to maintain the church polity and various ranks of the ecclesiastical hierarchy." The traditional canonical provision was for bishops to ordain, though exceptions could be and had been made in emergencies. And what about apostolic succession? Yes, we confess the apostolicity of the church through the centuries, calling for ongoing agreement in the apostolic faith and in the apostolic preaching. Within this apostolic succession of the church in faith and doctrine is continuity in the apostolic ministry. We know that three things emerged virtually together at the same time in the early church: the apostolic canon, the apostolic creed, and the apostolic ministry. Evangelical catholics say we must take all three, for they are inseparably interlinked. We know, of course, that the apostles did not write the entire New Testament; they did not write the Apostles' Creed. Yet we believe and confess the canon and the creed to be apostolic. When we have figured that out, the same logic holds for the apostolicity of the ministry, even though we cannot demonstrate that every bishop, presbyter, and deacon in the early church was ordained by one of the apostles.

This sort of evangelical catholic reading of the Confessions actually prevailed in most of the ecumenical dialogues, leading to optimistic claims of far-reaching convergence if not consensus on the understanding of ministry with many partner churches, including the Roman Catholic. The USA Lutheran-Catholic Dialogue stated, for example: "The episcopal structure and polity of the Roman Catholic church does not in itself constitute a problem for the Lutherans. Indeed, the Book of Concord itself affirms the desire of the Lutheran reformers to preserve, if possible, the episcopal polity that they had inherited from the past."[23] The Lutheran dialoguers conclude their statement by saying: "We recommend to those who have appointed us that through appropriate channels the participating Lutheran churches be urged to declare formally their judgment that the ordained ministries of the Roman Catholic Church are engaged in a valid ministry of the gospel."[24] Perhaps more importantly, after marshalling historical and theological arguments the Catholic team affirmed that Roman Catholics should no longer "continue to question the eucharistic presence of the Lord in the midst of the Lutherans when they meet to celebrate the Lord's Supper. . . . We see no persuasive reason to deny the possibility of the Roman Catholic Church recognizing the validity of this ministry. Accordingly we ask the authorities of the Roman Catholic Church whether the ecumenical urgency flowing from Christ's will for unity may not dictate that the Roman Catholic church recognize the validity of the Lutheran ministry."[25]

The evangelical catholic understanding of ministry, ordination, and succession is further to be found in the two documents on ministry published by the International Roman Catholic/Lutheran Joint Commission. The two documents are, *The Gospel and the Church* (Malta Report, 1972) and *Ministry in the Church* (1981). Perhaps the boldest proposal for a mutual recognition of ministries came out of the work of the Groupe de Dombes. This ecumenical study group, founded in 1937 by a French theologian, P. Couturier,[26] was composed of forty Lutheran, Reformed, and Catholic theologians from France and Switzerland. In 1972 and 1973 they published two consensus documents on the eucharist and the ministry. They announced their stunning conviction that there remains no fundamental disagreement on the nature and significance of the special ministry, and though certain difficulties remain on both sides with regard to the structuring of the offices, these difficulties no longer need to be deemed church-dividing. The work of the Groupe de Dombes has enjoyed extraordinary influence in later ecumenical dialogues, and has been undoubtedly a major source of inspiration behind the Lutheran-Catholic publication, *Facing Unity*, which constructs a scenario of ways and means to achieve church fellowship between Lutherans and Catholics.

---

23. Eucharist and Ministry, *Lutherans and Catholics in Dialogue*, IV, 1970, p. 19.
24. *Lutherans and Catholics in Dialogue*, IV, 1970, p. 22.
25. *Lutherans and Catholics in Dialogue*, IV, 1970, p. 31.
26. Couturier was the proponent of the Week of Prayer for Christian Unity.

This evangelical catholic reading of Lutheran identity has proved to be ecumenically fruitful. It has found expression not only in the Lutheran-Catholic dialogues and the Lutheran-Orthodox dialogues, especially between the Finnish Lutherans and Russian Orthodox, but also in the Porvoo Agreement between Nordic Lutherans and Anglicans of the British Isles as well as in the Concordat of Agreement between the Evangelical Lutheran Church in America and the Episcopal Church USA, behind both of which lies the Niagara Report.

Those who successfully defeated the passage of the Concordat knew what they were doing: they were taking a stand against the evangelical catholic vision of the ecumenical destiny of Lutheranism. But what should not be forgotten is that almost two-thirds of the delegates voted for the Concordat, which would have paved the way for Lutherans to accept the threefold office of ministry and the historic episcopate — the very linchpin in further ecumenical rapprochement on the ordained ministry between the churches still separated.

All shades of opinion continue to be held on matters of ministry, doctrinal and practical. Various factions remain in contention. Some still hold the transference theory, with its low view of the ordained ministry. Some of these even claim that for church unity the Confessions affirm the necessity of only word and sacraments, by whomsoever they happen to be administered. Others hold out for a single office of ordained ministry, which means only pastors, not bishops and deacons. A coalition of pietists and confessionalists, who certainly don't agree with each other, found common ground at Philadelphia in 1997 in their opposition to the Concordat and its provision for episcopacy. All this proves is that the legacy of ambiguity on ministry lives on, and where it will lead nobody knows.

Conclusion

We must end in the middle of the story. American Lutheranism remains impaled on the horns of a dilemma on ministry, along with other churches in the Protestant tradition. It was the issue of ministry on which the ten Protestant denominations in COCU — the Consultation of Church Union — got hung up. Nobody knows how to fix what broke in the sixteenth century. Yet the ecumenical movement remains the best and really the only laboratory in which to explore and experiment with models that lead to reconciliation and unity. The Lutheran experience in the ecumenical dialogues has led to convergence with the Great Tradition on ministry, ordination, and succession, helping Lutherans to recall and retrieve the catholic substance of their confessional tradition. But other forces are also at work that pull in opposite directions. Some are working to keep Lutheranism prisoner in its mighty fortress, voicing opposition to the current "full communion" agreements, as well as to the more far-reaching agreement with Catholics on justification by faith. Others would draw Lutheranism further into the vortex of pan-evangelical Protestantism, whose links to the classical Orthodox and Catholic traditions are weak or nonexistent. The ordained ministry is being hammered also on the cultural front. Recent studies of social scientists suggest that we as a culture tend to remove every structure of authority — human or divine — from our lives so that the final criterion is the sovereign self. What is good for me, what makes me feel good, dictates what matters in religion and morality.[27] The *sensus fidelium* is determined by the "habits of the heart," by gut feelings. In place of scriptural, creedal, sacramental, and institutional authorities we are left with a democracy of equally valid private opinions.

So what if we lose the spiritual authority of the ministry, mediated within the church and signified by ordination? May we not still fall back on the authority of the Bible and take our stand there? But the appeal to biblical authority also dissolves in the acids of this cultural critique of authority, and is replaced by the competing opinions of scholars who remove the historical-critical method from its original ecclesial context. The whole house of authority collapses, on whatever foundation it claims to stand.

The contemporary attack against the recovery of the threefold office of ministry, a sacramental understanding of ordination, and apostolic succession, claims to be based on the New Testament and the Confessions. But we have shown that this is true only if we discount the "early catholicism" of the Pastoral Epistles and only if we read the Confessions through Protestant eyes, with a Protestant hermeneutic. One theologian has recently written: "Christians are called as the church: the democracy of the justified. In this fundamental teaching Lutherans, along with the Protestant tradition generally, stand opposed to the strong emphasis in Catholic doctrine that identifies the church as a guaranteed visible struc-

27. In a debate in St. Mark's Cathedral in Minneapolis with Canon Joel Gibson, former Governor Al Quie said: "The historic episcopate is not important. I don't believe in it." That settles it! This is an example of the level of debate on the ministry that prevailed at the 1997 Philadelphia assembly of the ELCA, on the part of both clergy and laity.

ture in the world by means of ecclesiastical hierarchy in general and the episcopal office in particular."[28] The scare words are "guaranteed" and "hierarchy."

Bultmann rightly taught that every interpretation involves certain presuppositions. The presuppositions at work in the current crusade against the church's traditional ministry come not from the Reformation, for which the loss was a regrettable tragedy, but from the Enlightenment, for which it was a matter of good riddance, and thus, not from the normative sources of Christian dogmatics, but from modern concepts of individual freedom and personal autonomy.

The spirit of Schleiermacher and not Luther is the mastermind behind the denominational Lutheran resistance to recoup what was lost in the sixteenth century. It is ideology, not theology. Consider Schleiermacher's views on ministry: "No individual or small group of individuals can represent Christ: all the more must we regard this transference of offices as deriving solely from the whole body, and the formation of the clergy into a self-contained and self-propagating corporation has no Scriptural basis of any kind."[29] Schleiermacher did not view the Reformation as a reform and renewal movement within the Western church but as the beginning of a distinctively new type of Christianity. The two are antithetical. He stated: "The antithesis between Protestantism and Catholicism may provisionally be conceived thus: the former (Protestantism) makes the individual's relation to the Church dependent on his relation to Christ, while the latter (Catholicism) makes contrariwise the individual's relation to Christ dependent on his relation to the Church."[30] The assumption is that Christ and his church may be so separated, that you can have a Käsemannless body and a bodiless head. I prefer Anders Nygren's statement: "Christ and his Church are inseparable entities. Just as the Church is nothing without Christ, so also Christ is nothing without his Church."[31] And thus in the same book Nygren says that "as Christ is a part of the gospel, so also is his Church. The gospel about Christ is also the gospel about

28. Walter Sundberg, "Ministry in Nineteenth Century European Lutheranism," *Called and Ordained,* pp. 88-89.

29. Friedrich Schleiermacher, *The Christian Faith,* trans. and ed. by H. R. Mackintosh and James S. Stewart (Edinburgh: T. & T. Clark, 1928), p. 615.

30. *The Christian Faith,* p. 103.

31. Anders Nygren, *Christ and His Church,* trans. by Alan Carlsten (Philadelphia: Westminster Press, 1956), p. 90.

32. *Christ and His Church,* p. 30.

his Church."[32] Apostolicity is an attribute of this church. The church the apostles left behind is equipped with their authority; there is a continuing succession of the apostolic ministry of the gospel through the centuries to the present time. That gospel includes inseparably Christ and his church. This is the permanent bedrock foundation of the ordained ministry.

The French have a saying: *il faut reculer pour mieux avancer.* (To better move forward you must go back.) Experience teaches us that we cannot fix the theological problem of the ministry internal to our tradition by remaining within it. For the depth and breadth — the roots and branches — of the problem include how we relate to others who are part of the body of Christ. The body cannot heal itself one member at a time. The relationships are organic and holistic in nature. Generation after generation of Lutherans have tried again and again to find the magic key to the puzzle in Luther or the Confessions or some other Golden Age. It has not worked. We must return more deeply into the sources of the Great Tradition which provided the substance of their theological and spiritual life. We must find common ground in the deeper historic catholic and orthodox tradition — the tradition of the undivided church of the first millennium that transmitted to us the Scriptures, the creeds, the sacraments, the liturgies, the ministries, and through these means the very life-giving and Spirit-bestowing gospel itself — and therein find the foundation and framework for reaching the unity of churches in full communion that "all the king's horses and all the king's men couldn't put back together again."

Bringing Wittenberg and Geneva and Canterbury into a new arrangement of reconciled communities and ministries — of altar and pulpit fellowship — may be a good thing for the time being, but we need to keep looking simultaneously to the wider horizon of Christian unity that includes reconciliation between Rome and Constantinople, and finally all of the churches with them. For the unity we claim as individual Christians and churches to have in Christ entails communion with each other, and that communion necessarily calls for special forms of ecclesial life, including a common ordained ministry jointly exercised in eucharistic fellowship.

CATECHESIS

Catechesis for Our Time

ROBERT W. JENSON

I

I began teaching in 1955, in a liberal arts college of the church. My students were mostly fresh from active participation in their home town Protestant congregations. In those days, I and others like me regarded it as our duty, precisely for the sake of students' faith, to loosen them up a bit. They had been drilled in standard doctrine — Jesus is the Son of God, God is triune but what that means is a mystery, heaven is the reward of a good life — to the point of insensibility to the gospel itself.

In 1966 I left undergraduate teaching. Then just 23 years later, I returned to teach at a similar churchly liberal arts college. My students were again mostly fresh from active participation in Protestant congregations — though now with more Catholics mixed in. During those years, the situation exactly reversed itself.

It is now my duty to inform these young Christians that, e.g., there once was a man named Abraham who had an interesting life, that then there was Moses and that he came before Jesus, that Jesus was a Jew who is thought by some to be risen from the dead, that there are commandments claiming to be from God, and that they frown on fornication and such, and other like matters.

The great catechetical enterprises inaugurated by the Reformation and Counter-Reformation, in which parents, pastors, and congregational leaders undertook to equip people for participation in the church's life, have for the most part simply been dropped. Not enough remains of them

137

to make an interesting or productive subject for this lecture. Our thinking has to start from scratch.

"Catechetics" is the theory of "catechesis." "Catechesis" is what one does with "catechumens." And the existence of a group of people identified as "catechumens" is the mark of the church. The existence in the church of a group precisely of those being instructed, and the church's possession of a special terminology for them and for the activity of instructing them, should remind us that the church's instructional activities have their own specific origin. The church did not start to teach just because everyone does it, but because she had a specific need to do it, peculiar to her own life.

The church's "catechumens" were a specific group of people, named precisely from their position as those being instructed. The point of naming them that way was that they were not yet anything else, that this is all they *were* in the church, persons being instructed. The catechumens were persons brought to faith by the mission of the gospel, who nevertheless were not yet admitted to baptism and so not to the Supper. They were those being *prepared* for baptism and the Supper, for life in the church, and that was their very being so far as the church was concerned.

II

Now why did the ancient church decide converts needed such a period of preparation? Why did the ancient church posit *three kinds of people:* unbelievers, the baptized, and catechumens in between? In the New Testament itself, we read only of baptism immediately upon confession of faith; so the Ethiopian eunuch meets Philip, is told that Isaiah spoke of someone named Jesus, and is immediately baptized. But as it became apparent that generations had gone by without the Lord's return, so that the church had to suppose her history could go on for yet further generations, the church needed and was granted institutions that could sustain her faithfulness within continuing history. So the canon of Scripture emerged, and the episcopate in local succession, and creeds and rules of faith. And so also an *instructional* institution arose, situated between conversion and baptism.

For it was the experience of the church, after a bit of time had passed in which to have experience, that baptism and subsequent life in the liturgical and moral life of the church, if granted immediately upon hearing and affirming the gospel, were too great a shock for spiritual health. Life in the church was just too different from life out of the church, for people to tolerate the transfer without some preparation.

Converts were used to religious cults that had little moral content, that centered often on bloody sacrifice, and that were oriented — as we might now put it — to the "religious needs" of the worshiper. They were entering a cult oriented not to their religious needs but to the mandates of a particular and highly opinionated God. They were entering a cult centered around an unbloody and therefore nearly incomprehensible sacrifice. And most disorienting of all, they were entering a cult that made explicit moral demands. They needed to be coached and rehearsed in all that, if their conversion was to be sustainable.

III

Thus they needed to study, for a first thing, *liturgics*, that is, how to do these Christian things, so different from what could appeal to their existing habits and tastes. And they needed to be instructed in how to understand what they were doing.

And then there were those moral demands. Christian heads of household were not supposed to treat their wives as subjects, and both husband and wife were supposed to be sexually faithful — for converts from late-antique society such puritanism was a shocking violation of nature. More amazingly yet, Christian parents did not get rid of inconvenient children, not even of unborn ones. The list went on and on of things that converts' previous society regarded as *rights*, that the church regarded as *sins*. If converts were to stand up under all these infringements on their personal pursuits of happiness, they needed some time under the care of moral instructors and indeed of watchful moral disciplinarians.

And then there were those creeds and doctrines. New converts were used to religions with little specificity, and so with little intellectual content. You were expected to worship Osiris in Egypt and the Great Mother in Asia Minor and Dionysus in Greece, and all of them and a hundred others simultaneously in Rome, and if the theologies of these deities could not all be simultaneously true, no matter, since you were not anyway expected to take their myths seriously as knowledge. For a relatively trivial but historically pivotal case: Did you have to think that the notorious lunatic Caligula was in fact divine? Not really, just so long as you burnt the pinch of incense.

But with the Lord, the Father of Jesus, things were different. He insisted that you worship him exclusively or not at all. And that imposed a *cognitive* task: if you were to worship the Lord exclusively, you had to know *who he is,* you had to make identifying statements about him and intend these as statements of fact. You had to learn that in the same history occupied by Caesar or Alexander, the Lord had led Israel from Egypt and what that meant for the world. You had to learn that in the same history occupied by Tiberius one of his deputies had crucified an Israelite named Jesus and what that in sheer bloody fact meant for the world. You had to learn that this Jesus was raised from the dead, and try to figure out where he might now be located. It was a terrible shock for the religious inclusivists and expressivists recruited from declining antiquity. There was a whole library of texts to be studied and conceptual distinctions to be made, if new converts were in the long run to resist their culturally ingrained inclusivism and relativism.

Catechesis was born as the instruction needed to bring people from their normal religious communities to an abnormal one. That is, it was born as liturgical rehearsal and interpretation, moral correction, and instruction in a specific theology. Apart from need for these things, it is not apparent that the church would have had to *instruct* at all.

IV

And now we must turn from rehearsing sociology to recognizing a mystery, in Richard Norris's precise sense. Hidden in the catechumenate's liturgical and moral and theological instruction is nothing less than the church's knowledge of God. What the catechumenate initiates into is acquaintance with God.

In Judaism and Christianity we come to know God in the same way in which we come to know each other, by living our histories together. For the life of Israel and the church with God is the same sequence of events as the triune God's life with us. Thus the prayer of the church is not addressed to a monadic God, from a position external to him; it is addressed to the Father, with the Son and by the Holy Spirit. It is a discourse that belongs to the triune discourse by which God is God. Baptism and eucharist are not events merely in *our* sanctification; they are events in the life by which God himself is righteous. God's moral word to us, his *torah,* is not another word than that which is a second identity of his own life.

As we live the church's life, we live in the *totus Christus,* as a communal whole that is in fact, whatever might have been, the second identity of the Trinity. We live in the triune community as we live in various human communities. And we learn to know God in his community as we learn to know one another in our human communities. It is into nothing less than this acquaintance with God that the catechumenate initiates.

V

The so-called Constantinian settlement, which made Christianity the established religion of the culture, brought a flood of converts, many dubiously motivated. The endeavor to deal with these initially created a clearly formalized catechumenate, which followed the lines just described. But eventually it also destroyed the catechumenate altogether. For when the culture's religion and morality and the church's religion and morality are supposed to be more or less the same, no drastic measures will be taken to bring folk from the one to the other. The near-universality of infant baptism is the pivot; you cannot prepare someone to be baptized if she or he already is. So long as infant baptism was only one option, and predicated on the accomplished catechetical discipline of the parents, the catechumenate could coexist with the practice. But when the parents themselves have been baptized as infants, the catechumenate loses its space.

And yet the church never got rid of the feeling that she *ought* to be catechizing, that there *is* a difference between her and the world, however culturally Christianized the latter, so that there is need for instruction in the difference. Of course, when nearly everybody was already baptized, the instruction had to take place *after* baptism, and be somehow motivated there. The junctures of life at which such instruction was undertaken, and its liturgical or other communal contexts, have varied wildly, as has the success of the efforts; in the not-too-distant past of much of Protestantism, this was done by making it a second condition of admission to the eucharist.

We come to our own situation. The Constantinian settlement has been disintegrating for two hundred years, and is now manifestly a thing of the past. Western civilization is still defined by Christianity, but in a strange way: the West now defines itself as the civilization that *used* to be Christian; the West is the civilization whose religion would be Christianity if it had any; the West, indeed, is the civilization so hung up on the Christianity it no longer believes, that its very life depends on attacking that Christianity. So, for a trivial example, last week Blanche Jenson and I attended a production at Minnesota's premier cultural institution, the Guthrie theater in Minneapolis. The play was David Hare's *Racing Demon,* which exposes the "corruption and hypocrisy" of the Church of England. Estimates of the play's worth may vary. My present point is this: Can you imagine a theater like the Guthrie staging a play that got its kicks by exposing the inner corruption and hypocrisy of, perhaps, North American shamanism? Only think of all those pious Minnesotan church-goers, sitting there happily laughing at the church, who if it had been any other religion being mocked would have marched out of the theater in a moment and started a campaign to fire the director.

So to my immediate point. The church in the West can no longer suppose that the regular schools or the organs of public opinion or the institutions of the arts or sciences instruct people in a way that is harmonious with the church's instruction. Indeed, we must assume the contrary: that they will inculcate ideological naturalism, moral relativism, and the superiority of all other religions to Christianity.

The church's catechetical institutions are in ruins because we have not in practice fully recognized this situation. What we must understand is that we have, in most respects, returned to the situation of the ancient church. Now as then, those to be integrated into the life of the church come from an alien culture; the church's life is a shock and a puzzlement for them, and sharing it is a nearly unsustainable strain. *The catechumenate is again mandated in its original function and intent.*

Our situation of course differs from that of the ancient church in one way, which makes a desperate complication: most of these heathen whom catechesis should prepare for life in the church are already in it and suppose themselves already to believe. During the time while the church is still coming to consciousness of its post-Constantinian situation, and just beginning to accept the obligations of its new sectarian status, such confusion is obviously to be anticipated.

Much of the American church has capitulated to the confusion. It is by now a platitude: much of the American Protestant Church, and now in belated and lamentable imitation much of the Catholic Church also, has tried to maintain its cultural position by minimizing the differences, that is, by minimizing its own character as church. If the world will no longer let the church set the agenda, much of the American church has tried to maintain its cultural place by asking the world to set *its* agenda.

Congregations and denominations that have gone any considerable distance down that road do not of course need to take any very drastic catechetical measures, there being nothing in their lives to prepare anyone for. If a congregation's service is a concert of popular religious music, with perhaps a homily on "love" or some other favorite delusion of the culture, those drawn to attend will need no special training. A religious conclave that is as enthusiastic for fornication as the public schools, or as supportive of the killing of innocents as the National Organization of Women, can dispense with moral teaching and discipline. A supposed church that proclaims that all gods justify has no need of theology.

But let us suppose that our congregations have remained to some degree faithful. That therefore the gap between what they do and think and what the culture does and thinks grows daily wider. And that therefore they do the catechumenate. What would it teach? I will adduce the same trio as before: liturgy, morals, and theology.

VI

We begin with liturgy. The culture has accustomed people to religious exercises that express, and then nourish, their individual religious needs and experiences. As a delegate to a recent convention of the ELCA put it, pleading for fellowship with more or less everybody, "I am a Lutheran because that kind of church suits my personal relation with God. Other people have their different relations with God, and so need other kinds of churches. We must just love each other."

The church has the daunting task of integrating persons so acculturated into the ritual life of a community that has her own identity, a community that is what she is whatever the personal religiosities of her members, in that her life is determined by the specific reality of a specific God. Recently I talked to a pastors' group about the minimal biblical mandates for celebration of the eucharist. When I had finished, a pastor's wife objected, "But what difference does any of this make, if what we do satisfies people's religious needs?" That is indeed how the culture thinks, and if the church is to continue as church, she must set her face like flint against it.

The Christian church has rites that she is not permitted to change: she initiates into her fellowship by washing in the triune name of her specific God; she is to maintain the telling of a specific message, that the God of Israel — and none other — has raised his servant Jesus — and none other — from the dead; she has her own identity as she offers a sacrifice of praise and thanksgiving for Jesus, to his Father, invoking their Spirit, with sharing of bread and the cup of wine. She is not permitted to adapt these things to the antecedent needs or prejudices of the uninstructed. So, for example, people in our culture fear germs the way antique peoples feared demons, but the church may not therefore disobey the Lord who told us, "All of you, drink out of it." People in our culture do not like to hear of redemptive suffering, except in the most sentimental sense, but the church may not therefore preach of other things than the Cross. People in our culture are so analytically turned in on themselves, that some of them indeed convince themselves that they suffered too much from their fathers to be baptized into "Father, Son, and Spirit," but the church may not therefore baptize otherwise. Etcetera.

Instead of perverting her essential rites, the church must catechize. She must *rehearse* her would-be members in the liturgies, take them through them step by step, showing how the bits hang together, and teaching them how to say or sing or dance them. And she must show them wherein these rites are blessings and not legal impositions.

Nor does it stop with the minimal mandates of Scripture. The church, like every living community, has her own interior culture, built up during the centuries of her history. That is, the acts of proclamation and baptism and eucharist are in fact embedded in a continuous tradition of ritual and diction and music and iconography and interpretation, which constitutes a churchly culture in fact thicker and more specific than any national or ethnic culture.

Now of course this tradition might have been different than it is. If the church's first missionary successes had taken her more south than west, her music and architecture and diction and so on would surely have developed differently. And in the next century, when the center of the church's life will probably indeed be south of its original concentration, the church's culture will continue to develop, and in ways that cannot now be predicted. But within Christianity, what might have been is beside the point; contingency is for Christianity the very principle of meaning; it is what in fact has happened — that might not have happened — that is God's history with us, and so the very reality of God and of us.

We are not, therefore, permitted simply to shuck off chant and chorale, or the crucifix, or architecture that encloses us in biblical story, or ministerial clothing that recalls that of ancient Rome and Constantinople, or so on and on. Would-be participants will indeed find some of this off-putting; people will indeed drift into our services, not grasp the proceedings, and drift out again. We will be tempted to respond by dressing in t-shirts and hiring an almost-rock group — not, of course, a real one — and getting rid of the grim crucifixes. Then we will indeed need less catechesis to adapt would-be participants to the church, *because* we will be much less church. If instead we are aware of the mission, and of the mission's situation in our particular time, we will not try to adapt the church's culture to seekers, but seekers to the church's culture.

So, for an only apparently trivial example, it is almost universally thought that children must be taught childish songs, with which occasionally to interrupt the service and serenade their parents. They are not, it is supposed, up to the church's hymns and chants. The exact opposite is the truth, and in any case the necessity. In my dim youth rash congregational officials once hired me to supervise the music program of a summer church school. I taught the children the ditties supplied me, but also some plain chant. When in the last days, I asked the children what they wanted to sing, it was always the plain chant.

Catechesis for our time, as the culture of the world and the culture of the church go separate ways, will be music training and art appreciation and language instruction, for the *church's* music and art and in the language of Canaan. If we do not do such things, and with passionate intention, the church will be ever more bereft of her own interior culture and just so become ever more the mere chaplaincy of the world's culture. The recommendations of the "church growth" movement will indeed produce growth, but not of the church.

VII

And then again the mystery. When we teach would-be believers how to do the church's liturgy, how to live in the fellowship of the church, we initiate them into nothing less than the eternal fellowship of the triune God. In that fellowship, they will learn to know God as they learn to know each other. When we teach would-be believers how to worship, we teach them to know God.

145

VIII

We turn to the church's odd morality. The culture, and so would-be Christians, are used to a morality of rights. And there is no denying that the notion of certain inalienable human rights is a necessary one — for that matter, it derives straight from medieval scholastic theology.

Nevertheless, the church's morality is fundamentally a morality not of rights but of opportunities for service, of permissions to love in risky ways that, were Christ not risen, would be merely imprudent. There is no avoiding it: insofar as the moral structure of would-be participants in the church's life is shaped by what now passes in the culture for morality, their moral structure must be disassembled and reassembled on a new pattern.

The culture is of course in moral crisis, as it must be since it has ceased to credit the Scriptures which created and supported its morality; this point has been much analyzed in recent years and there is no need for me to rehearse it here. The moral crisis of the culture presses its life-or-death issues on the church, as the church's people also must not only govern their own behavior with respect to them, but take their positions about them. You all know what these life-or-death matters are: the heterosexual monogamous family's normative position in society; the unborn human infant's protection from those for whom its death is advantageous, personally or as a source of employment; and now the suffering adult's similar protection.

We need not here decide how the sexual lives of those who call themselves homosexual should be socialized. But the church must resist the argument that because they have the same "right" to happiness, according to their own definition of it, as do others, that therefore the societally and legally paradigmatic position of the heterosexual family is an injustice that must be removed. The argument is perfectly valid, within the thinking of any who do not know how and for what God creates humanity. But the church, having read *Genesis*, knows that the distinction of male and female is constitutive for human being, and that the distinction is not a matter of orientations or desires, willed or not, but of sheer plumbing, of the mere shape of the bodies by which we are directed to each other. Would-be members of the church will mostly not know about the divinely ordained reality of sex; they must be instructed.

It is said that each individual woman has "reproductive rights," that is, the "right" to do with her body as she autonomously chooses, and to do the same with what within her body results from what she does with it. It is

146

further said that she has the right also to summon the resources of the society to assist her in carrying out these rights. The unborn child, it is sometimes granted, may also have rights; but these must surely give way before the rights of the already adult participant in society. Again, the argument is valid *if* human society is a congeries of autonomous individuals held together only by procedural structures. But the church knows that even fallen human society is not quite such a hell. The starting point of all justice and all humanity is the recognition that one's own body is the very thing over which one does *not* have autonomous rights, since it is intended by God as the reality of our presence to *each other*. And every child, however conceived, is a miraculous new gift of God, to be received at whatever other cost. People do not know these things; if they want to be part of the church, they have to be taught and acknowledge them.

It is said that every sufferer has a right not to suffer if she or he does not want to, and that if this cannot be achieved without killing the sufferer, she or he has a right to have that done. But here above all no one can conceivably have such a right. We may not kill for private advantage, not even ourselves — not if there is God whose breath *is* the life of every human. Assuredly physicians may not kill for private advantage, in the course of their practice. The case here is so simple that little argument is needed or indeed possible; a society where the matter seemed difficult or subtle would already have approached very close to the condition of hell.

IX

And yet again the mystery. It is a piece of ecumenically received theology: between God's will and God personally there is no final difference. To instruct in the commandments is to introduce to God.

X

Finally there is theology. Folk are baptized into the name — that is, worship of and obedience to — a specific God. They have to know who that is. He is not Moloch, and therefore he does not want the blood of our children. He is not the Goddess, and therefore does not reveal himself in polymorphous sexuality. He is not the spirit of the wolf, and therefore dreams of wolves are not divine revelation. He is neither the Dialectic of History nor the Invisible Hand of the free market, and therefore life cannot be fulfilled by economic endeavor of whatever sort. And so on and on.

For my students, it is always a revelation that there are many and decidedly different candidates for the God-job, and that all of them cannot simultaneously be legitimate. Once the logic of the matter is pointed out to them, they see it. But somehow, their pastors and church teachers had not pointed it out to them.

The God of the church is Father, Son, and Spirit. For persons able to learn, warranted participation in the church's life requires fairly precise knowledge of the doctrine of the Trinity. This should not in fact require much time to teach; the time required is inversely proportional to the depth and accuracy of the teacher's knowledge.

Then, of course, since the church will be baptizing and making eucharist, those able to learn need to understand something of what the church thinks it is doing when it does these things. And again, the time required to give adequate understanding is inversely proportional to the depth of the teacher's understanding.

XI

One more time the mystery. We first need to know who God is in order to address him. The doctrine of Trinity — and indeed, by derivation, all Christian teaching — is not in the first instance a discourse in the third person, but rather in the second. It is in the first instance doxology, and only secondarily description. Therefore, when we teach would-be believers doctrine, we teach them to intrude on God.

XII

You will not think I have fulfilled my assignment if I say nothing about how and when such instruction is to be done. And I am in fact going to disappoint you. So long as the church and Western culture are still separating but not fully separated, confusion between the church and the culture is unavoidable. Those who most desperately need catechizing will mostly be persons who see no such necessity. The intake of new members will be a mix of adult converts and children of old members presented for baptism. Of the latter, some will be legitimately presented and most will not be. In the situation, all you can do is play catch as catch can. All you can do is be alert for occasions and places in your particular situation, where a bit of needed catechesis can be slipped in. For the most part, all one can talk about in advance, as I have tried to do, is what it is for which we are seeking occasion, so as to recognize occasion when it appears.

But I do have three modest particular proposals. One is especially made to those who may happen to have or be able to acquire some denominational influence. Quite apparently, a prime group of persons who need drastic catechizing is candidates for the ordained ministry. Particularly the clergy's moral formation has obviously been inadequate, and in the very area where the culture's moral collapse most desperately needs to be resisted — the area of sexual practice. I do not suppose seminaries can be made to do it, but if they really wanted to prepare persons for ordination, they would devote great energy — not to classroom teaching in "Christian ethics" — but to the direct daily moral training of their students.

A second suggestion has already been made in David Yeago's chapter. So let me merely encourage the various programs now called "adult catechumenates."

And then there is a place where, with sufficient courage, action could in many congregations be taken tomorrow. We cannot catechize infants presented for baptism. And probably no one will get up the amount of courage needed to reject presented infants wholesale. But it *could* be made a requirement of infant baptism, that the *parents* or other primary caretakers undergo a catechumenate before the child is baptized.

XIII

We baptize into God. Baptism must be carried by catechesis. Thus we catechize into God.

DISCIPLESHIP

On Making Disciples of the Lord Jesus Christ

WILLIAM J. ABRAHAM

Introduction

Let me begin with a vignette from my own experience.

On my way to this conference, my initial flight was canceled, and I had to take a taxi. Usually on occasions like this I am content to sit back and relax, but in this instance I got into a long conversation with the taxi driver. The story that unfolded was fascinating. He had had no serious Christian background. His parents were divorced. His mother had been a Roman Catholic; his father did not really believe in anything. At the age of fifteen, during a period of difficulty in his life, he had stumbled onto and read a Gideon Bible. The only thing he could remember is that he had a strange feeling in reading the portion of Scripture that he read — a feeling of peace.

In due course, he started visiting various churches. After visiting several and mulling over what he had seen, he arrived at an interesting decision. He decided to be a good person, become rich, and then he would be in a position to join one of the churches. Happily, when he told this to a distant cousin, he was informed that this inference from his observations would not hold. He was told that he needed to ask Jesus into his heart and then to ask God to help him, and after that he would become a good person. In the meantime he should get baptized and join the local Baptist church. And this is what he did. He later married a Roman Catholic woman, and eventually joined a Lutheran church. He is now trying to figure out why the minister at his Lutheran church was reading from a new translation of the Bible, and is convinced that the modern translation is an illegitimate interpretation. He is also trying to figure out why Baptists frown on drinking and dancing, while Lutherans permit both drinking and dancing. For his part he does not drink, but he does like to dance, but only with his wife; he thinks it is dangerous to dance with anyone other than your wife.

We can't help being struck by the delightful tenacity of this pilgrim. He has been a believer for many years, yet he is still driven in part by his experience of reading a Gideon Bible as a teenager. Perhaps more importantly for our purposes today, we are struck by the difficulty he encountered in finding anyone to introduce him to the essentials of Christian faith. It's if he became a disciple of Jesus Christ by default.

Discipleship and the Marks of the Church

It is surely one of the enduring puzzles of the contemporary American church that so many people wander in and out of its communities and buildings without ever finding their feet as healthy disciples of Jesus Christ. What does this signify? Does it mean that the church forfeits its right to be seen as a church? If discipleship is a mark of the church, then it would appear that we must answer this in the affirmative. This is a startling proposal within most of mainline Protestantism down through its history. We immediately associate discipleship as a mark of the church with Anabaptism and other like-minded groups; and these we naturally think of as sectarian bodies committed to a conception of the church as a voluntary association of true believers. Our list of the marks of the church rarely stretches that far. We think of either two marks of the church: the preaching of the word and the right administration of the sacraments; or four marks of the church: unity, holiness, catholicity, and apostolicity. In neither of these cases do we think naturally of discipleship. To bring in discipleship would draw us away from the idea of the church as a thoroughly mixed bag of believers and unbelievers, of saints and sinners, of wheat and chaff, who can only be separated at the last judgment.

I am thinking of discipleship here in relatively restricted terms, that is, in terms of taking up one's cross and following Jesus Christ. The disciple from this point of view is one who suffers in a way that echoes the suffering of the Lord. Thus the Christian life is one of self-denial; it involves a radical obedience to the will of God which takes precedence over one's personal interests; equally it involves bearing the opposition and resistance of the world, if need be to the point of death. Clearly this is a prominent theme in the Gospels, and it is magnificently made manifest in the lives of the saints and martyrs of the church.

The complexity of the discipleship involved is often best captured by new converts. Consider this splendid description given by a former chief Rabbi of Rome, Eugenio Zolli.

> The *Follow me* was an invitation to follow the master completely. The patriarchs walked before God; Christ's followers follow Christ, in Christ; and this opened to me the way to understand the mystery of the Mystical Body of Christ. The follower becomes a living and active cell in the Mystical Body, the Church of Christ. It is a *communion,* a bond which transcends the relation of blood and nation. Conversion is therefore thought of as baptism, rebirth, a second birth in the person, life, works — and above all in the death — of Christ. All things were new and interesting; not the least interesting was the conception of the Beyond, not as a great academy where the masters study the Law under the presidency of the Lord, and where Moses, hearing how he is quoted, does not recognize his text. The life of the Beyond is joy in Christ; it is the continuation of the spiritual symposium begun on earth, in the midst of sufferings, sacrifices, martyrdom. In heaven the communion with Christ becomes pure joy. We suffer, then we rejoice; we rise in Christ to live with Christ.[1]

Zolli subtly brings together here discipleship, conceived as following Christ, with membership in the church, that is, with being a living cell in the Mystical Body.

One theologian who goes so far as to make discipleship a mark of the church is none other than Martin Luther. For Luther, discipleship is the last item in a list of seven marks of the church. The first six are, in order: possession of the holy Word of God; the sacrament of baptism; the sacrament of the altar; the offices of the keys exercised publicly; the possession of consecrated ministers; and the offering of prayer, public praise, and thanksgiving to God.[2] The seventh mark follows and is worth quoting in full.

---

1. Eugenio Zolli, *Why I Became a Catholic* (Harrison, New York: Roman Catholic Books, n.d.). The original title to this book was *Before the Dawn,* a much more apt title, for the book is more about the journey to Christ than it is the journey to Rome.

2. Luther adds further signs of the church which are moral in nature but which are placed at a level below these seven signs.

. . . the holy Christian people are externally recognized by the holy possession of the cross. They must endure every misfortune and persecution, all kinds of trials and evil from the devil, the world, and the flesh (as the Lord's prayer indicates) by inward sadness, timidity, fear, outward poverty, contempt, illness, and weakness, in order to become like their head, Christ. And the only reason they must suffer is that they steadfastly adhere to Christ and God's Word, enduring this for the sake of Christ, Matthew 5[:11], "Blessed are you when men persecute you on my account." They must be pious, quiet, obedient, and prepared to serve the government and everybody with life and goods, doing no one any harm. No people on earth have to endure such bitter hate; they must be accounted worse than Jews, heathen, and Turks. In summary, they must be called heretics, knaves, and devils, the most pernicious people on earth, to the point where those who hang, drown, murder, torture, banish, and plague them to death are rendering God a service. No one has compassion on them; they are given myrrh and gall to drink when they thirst. And all this is done not because they are adulterers, murderers, thieves, or rogues, but because they want to have none but Christ, and no other God. Wherever you see or hear this, you may know that the holy Christian church is there, as Christ says in Matthew 5[:11-12], "Blessed are you when men revile you and utter all kinds of evil against you on my account. Rejoice and be glad for your reward is great in heaven." This too is a holy possession whereby the Holy Spirit sanctifies his people, but also blesses them.[3]

The wider context of Luther's comment is important. His remarks crop up in a pungent essay on the nature and significance of church councils. Luther is at pains to work out a substantial and coherent vision of the church to replace the corruption he saw all around him. His project is one of reforming and re-creating the church; he is not here, if he ever was, interested in the issue of the logic and practice of evangelization. Yet his discussion is illuminating. Discipleship for Luther cannot be separated from the church; this is the crucial point to be noted. Discipleship is one element in a very thick description of the church. Hence to become a disciple is not simply to take on board a way of living, as if we could isolate cross-bearing and suffering in an act of heroic decision as a badge of personal identity. To be a disciple is to take on board a way of living in a community

---

3. Eric W. Gritsch, ed., *Luther's Works,* vol. 41, *Church and Ministry III* (Philadelphia: Fortress, 1966), pp. 164-65.

that possesses a particular form and content. It is to be initiated into a very particular community marked by Scripture, sacrament, an ordered ministry, discipline, and worship. Moreover, as we know from the shape of Luther's theology as a whole, it is through the grace of God working in and through the sacraments and ministry of the church that discipleship is possible. Hence it is no accident that discipleship comes last on his list. Its location bears eloquent testimony to the primacy of the gospel and grace in the economy of Christian existence.

Discipleship, the Making of Disciples, and Apostolicity

I have already mentioned that Luther's thesis is a startling one. It appears not to have survived in the appropriation of Luther in the classical confessions of the Reformation period. What we have inherited is something that on the surface appears very different. The church is marked by Word and sacrament, or by unity, holiness, catholicity, and apostolicity. So where do we go from here? Should we scrap talk of discipleship in discussions of the marks of the church? Or should we go back to first principles and work through a fresh vision of the marks of the church which would reintroduce discipleship as a mark of the church? Or is there a way to unpack the standard ways of identifying the marks of the church which would allow us to take up the theme of discipleship in a natural and creative way?

The first solution, which is liable to ignore the deep insight buried in Luther's proposal, strikes me as a counsel of despair. The second solution is much too daunting in a short essay. Hence I am left to pursue the third. In doing so let's take as a given that the marks of Word and sacrament can readily be folded into the classical marks of the church as represented by unity, holiness, catholicity, and apostolicity. Thus it seems to me that Word and sacrament are readily involved in the claim that the church is apostolic. To be apostolic means in part to receive from the apostles the ministry of Word and sacrament. Does it not also mean that we succeed the apostles in following our Lord in two ways that connect automatically with the idea of discipleship? We follow the apostles truly both in *being* disciples of the Lord Jesus Christ and in *making* disciples of the Lord Jesus Christ. Luther is thus on to something of enormous significance. He is helping us unpack, however fitfully, the richness of the church in its apostolic identity. This is the deep insight buried in Luther's comment, and we ignore it at our peril.

I say "fitfully" here because I think that Luther is only half right. What is at stake is not just the life of discipleship but the ministry of making disciples. What is at issue is not just a moral imperative but also a missionary imperative. The church is not just called to be a body of disciples; it is also called to make disciples.

This shift of perspective is crucial, for it calls us to broaden the idea of discipleship beyond the one already deployed. Indeed, given the complex context in the church in which Luther embeds his idea of discipleship, it is clearly possible to broaden the concept of discipleship to cover those persons who are learning the full contours of the Christian faith. A disciple, on this analysis, is not just someone who is taking up the cross but taking up all that is to be learned from Jesus Christ as Lord and Savior. This broader notion of discipleship is clearly visible in the Great Commission text of Matthew. Here discipleship clearly entails being baptized into the apostolic community and being taught all that Jesus has taught the first disciples.

We have now come within sight of the last move I want to make before proceeding further. I began with a story that readily displays the struggle to be a disciple of Jesus Christ. What is striking about this story is that this development is not accidental. Hosts of people struggle with the life of discipleship because of the incompetence of the church in the art of making disciples in modern western culture. The church is weak in its discipleship because it is weak in the art of making disciples. Failure in discipleship is inevitable so long as the church fails to form its members adequately in discipleship. This is the problem that has to be tackled with resolution and flair. Hence the question I now want to pursue is this: What is at stake for the church today if it is to take the making or formation of discipleship seriously? Or put more sharply, what does it mean for the church to be engaged in the ministry of making disciples of Jesus Christ? Hence I am bold to make this topic — the art of making disciples — the focus of the rest of this paper. It is this aspect of apostolic identity that cries out for attention and analysis in our current situation.

I find myself thinking about this issue partly in a spirit of lament and partly in a spirit of cheerfulness. The lament is self-explanatory given the story recounted, for clearly we have a very mixed record as far as success in making disciples is concerned. The cheerfulness stems from a deep conviction that we have entered a period of incubation in the church in the West. I think that this is true generally in theology, but it is markedly true in the field of mission and evangelism. Thus we are in a period of intense but uncoordinated experiment in evangelism and catechesis. Aside from the conventional efforts in confirmation classes, churches are experimenting with special Bible study programs, courses in Basic Christianity, weekend retreats like Walk to Emmaus, short pilgrimages, new forms of catechesis as represented by the Rite of Christian Initiation for Adults, hosts of homespun church membership classes, and the like. Furthermore, for the first time in centuries, if ever, there is a serious theological conversation emerging on the nature and logic of evangelism. As part of this the complex history of evangelism is being recovered by fits and starts, most recently the great significance of the work of the Celtic monks in Europe after the dark ages.[4] To crown it all, at least one mainline church, the United Methodist Church, has accepted the making of disciples of Jesus Christ as its formally adopted mission statement.

Yet all of this remains a buzz of activity if we do not carefully think through what we are doing. Moreover, it is only as we think through these issues that we can see the force of insisting that the making of discipleship is truly a mark of the church. This may take us further afield than we may want to go, but it has the great merit of bringing home some of the practical consequences of taking with radical seriousness the place of discipleship in the identity of the church.

Three issues naturally spring to mind, as I think about the making of disciples. First, what images or concepts best sum up our work in making disciples? I shall call this the initiation question. Second, how do we relate to the questions and needs of those who seek to be disciples of Jesus Christ? I shall call this the content question. Third, what is the best form of pedagogy or spiritual direction for new disciples? I shall call this the pedagogical question.[5] Clearly I cannot begin to answer all these questions here, but I think I want to make substantial progress on the first two; and I am content today to comment briefly on the third. As we proceed I shall pause here and there to keep building the case of making disciples as a mark of the church.

---

4. For a fine treatment of this issue see John Finney, *Recovering the Past, Celtic and Roman Mission* (London: Darton, Longman & Todd, 1996).

5. We might approach the same network of issues in terms of traditional questions posed in cases of curriculum design: What are the objectives we should set ourselves in the making of disciples? What materials and practices do we need to engage or use? What methods should we implement?

The Logic of Initiation

How should we conceive of the art of making disciples? One obvious answer comes to mind immediately: To make disciples is to initiate people
into the church. In turn this vision provides the fundamental horizon for
guiding our choices concerning the content and logistics of disciple making. To complete the picture, we carefully unpack what it will take to bring
about effective initiation into the church. We provide, that is, a description
of the contours of initiation and an account of the practices required to secure their production. We must of course set all this in the context of the
mysterious working of the Holy Spirit in the church, for we are not talking
here of a secular initiation into a worldly institution, but with that crucial
qualification we are well on our way to answering one of the central questions posed above. We now know what it is to make disciples: to make disciples is to initiate people into the church.

This will appear so obvious and natural that it must look as if I am
carrying salmon to Seattle. There is, however, another way to move from
Luther to the contemporary situation. While Luther speaks eloquently of
the church here, his proposal is surely at odds with the massive failure of
the actual, empirical church in the West against which Luther so vehe-
mently protested. He was forced to argue as he did precisely because the
church had failed. His proposal required the reestablishment of the church
on appropriate foundations. This whole operation presupposes that there
is something prior to the church on which it can be founded and
refounded when it goes astray. He assumed that prior to the church there
was the coming of the Word in Christ; there was the appearance of the
kingdom in the life, death, and resurrection of Christ; there was the outpouring of the Spirit at Pentecost. This opens up the door to a very different way of conceiving the making of disciples. Would it not be better, it
will be asked, to locate discipleship not in the church, but in the kingdom
of God which gave birth to the church and to which it owes allegiance? On
this reading what we should pursue is not initiation into the church but
initiation into the kingdom of God. It is the kingdom that sets the agenda
for the content and logistics of the art of making disciples.

Resolving the tension between these two ways of thinking about the
location of discipleship has not received the attention it deserves. On the
first proposal, one enters the church and therein is formed and shaped into
a disciple. Here the church comes first logically and temporally. The main
argument in its favor is that without the church there is no discipleship. At

best there are a few heroic souls loosely connected to Christian communities who make it to the promised land as a holy remnant of rugged individuals. At worst there are aggregates of individuals forced to wander from pillar to post in the wilderness of modern culture and constantly eaten alive by its values and pressures. In the second proposal, one enters the kingdom and thereby becomes a disciple; as disciples join together, the church emerges as a happy by-product. In this scenario the kingdom comes first logically and temporally.[6] The church is a by-product of the arrival of the kingdom. At best the church is seen as a next step beyond becoming a disciple; at worst the church is seen as a snare, as corrupt, as a problem to be overcome or gotten around.[7] The crucial argument for this alternative is that initiation into the church is no guarantee of initiation into the kingdom. The church is too fragile in its faithfulness to be given pride of place in the logic of initiation.

Which of these two options should we choose? In my earlier efforts to think through this matter I opted for initiation into the kingdom over against initiation into the church.[8] I argued that we should focus on initiation into the kingdom and we should think of that initiation as necessarily involving initiation into the church. What is at issue here, of course, is a deep tension between ecclesiology and eschatology, between the church and the kingdom, as the center of gravity for our thinking about evangelism. I resolved the tension by giving primacy to the kingdom over the church. It seemed obvious to me that the kingdom was logically and temporally prior to the church and hence ought to be given the place of honor in my deliberations.[9] Given my background in Methodist circles I was naturally aware of the deep failure of the church to live up to its responsibilities in the area of making disciples, for Methodism was in part a movement which had arisen because the church refused to take evangelism

6. Most popular forms of evangelism have opted for this latter option without really addressing the issue. The call to discipleship is invariably presented in such a way that initiation into the church is an afterthought or a distraction.

7. One of the recurring laments one hears in evangelism is this: Where shall I take my friends once they decide to become disciples of Jesus Christ? The issue is effectively one of pastoral efficiency. Luther still had the confidence that he could locate or create the true church. Many despair of such confidence given the long history of claims and counterclaims concerning the identity of the true church.

8. See *The Logic of Evangelism* (Grand Rapids: Eerdmans, 1989).

9. I first became aware of this issue in extended conversation with Australian colleagues, especially Dean Drayton and Trevor Smith.

seriously. Furthermore, I wanted to be sensitive to the need for communities on the edge or even outside the church to make sure that this work was done. Moreover, I was acutely aware of how often the church either neglected the coming of the kingdom or domesticated the kingdom by reducing the kingdom to the life of the church.

On reflection I have come to have doubts about this way of resolving the dilemma I posed above. What we need here is not a choice between the church and the kingdom but a position which holds that both of these must be taken into consideration at once, and that when we do so we find that they complement each other in a deep way. My reasons for coming to doubt my earlier decision are these.

First, I have come to see that initiation into the church will require dealing with the same issues as is required when we deal with initiation into the kingdom, and vice versa. In both of these cases one starts from above, so to speak, seeking to spell out the varied character of the faith to be owned by the disciple. In both cases one must make a normative judgment about what it is to make disciples. But the normative task of the church can be described precisely as that of the initiation of people into the treasures of the kingdom. The church's job is not just to speak of itself but to speak of something beyond itself, even as it invites people to join its own ranks. Happily it makes little difference whether we deploy the concept of the kingdom or the concept of the church as the horizon of initiation. In each case we will have to make available the same kind of treasures and practices. The differences that surface at this point are cosmetic and verbal.

Second, and this complements the main point just made, I have come to see the tension between ecclesiology and eschatology as a bogus tension. While formally it is right to insist on a logical distinction between the church and the kingdom, contingently and in reality, there is no kingdom without a community, the church, and there is no church without the presence of the kingdom. God's reign has always had an Israel, an ecclesia, in history; it is not some sort of ahistorical, asocial reality. Equally the church would never have existed without the prior presence of the kingdom in history — in Israel, in Jesus Christ, and in Pentecost. So we need to find a better way to reflect this in our thinking about the making of disciples.

Third, while it is the case that the church often fails in its responsibilities, and there is, therefore, a need for ad hoc alternative arrangements in the economy of the gospel as represented by groups that operate on the edge or even outside the church, this sort of development is the exception that proves the rule. As we all know, relying on exceptions makes for bad law; it is unwise to argue from aberrations in the life of the faith to what should be normative in the life of the faith. My earlier decision rested implicitly on this false move. We need to acknowledge the failures and unfaithfulness of the church, but equally these should not be the deep ground of our thinking about the making of disciples. Our thinking should be grounded less on the wayward empirical realities of the church and more on a normative theological appraisal of her task and mission.

Fourth, to treat the church as just one dimension of entry into the kingdom is to underplay the place of the church in the work of making disciples. The life of the church is not just prudentially related to Christian discipleship; it is the place where one learns the very art of discipleship. Expressed more sharply, it is the church which is entrusted with the task of forming healthy disciples. It is the church which has been commissioned by God to proclaim the gospel of the kingdom to all the world, to call all people into discipleship, and to provide the crucial teaching and practices which are the marks of all true disciples of Jesus Christ. In short, it is the church which carries the right to identify the normative content of Christian initiation. Even in those cases where agents of the gospel may have to operate outside the boundaries of the church because of its corruption and sin, and even though we can rejoice that God uses such agents to achieve his good purposes, these agents are themselves dependent on the church for the resources of their decisions and practices.

The conclusion to which we are driving is now in sight. The primary task which *the church sets itself in making members is to initiate people into the kingdom of God* which has arrived in Jesus Christ through the working of the Holy Spirit. While the church through baptism and catechesis increases its membership, the work of the church in initiation is to point away from itself to a greater and more primordial reality, the kingdom of God. The church can fail in this. It can turn in on itself and invite people to become merely members of itself as a social institution in modern society. This can happen quite easily by intention; more often it happens by default. The results are obvious: hosts of baptized church members who have only minimally, if at all, been introduced to the great treasures of the kingdom of God. The solution to this problem is not to abandon the church and reach for the kingdom of God as an alternative. The solution is to recognize that the problem is ecclesiological: failure to focus on the kingdom is precisely a failure in ecclesiology. It is to ignore the fact that the church exists in and for service to the kingdom out of which it originated. It is the church which is commissioned by the risen Lord to make disciples who will be initiated into the glorious reality of God's reign on earth, a reality that is fully incarnate in Jesus Christ and made available through the work of the Holy Spirit. If it does not do this it is simply failing to be the church.

The Content of Initiation

It is now appropriate to take up the issue of the content of initiation. Here the question to be posed is this: What should we cover in the process of initiation if we are to be faithful to the normative decision just enumerated and if we are to be effective in the making of disciples? Both requirements need to be met. We need to work both from above, that is, the normative requirements of initiation, and from below, that is, the psychological requirements of initiation.

Consider an analogy. Imagine the work of a good music teacher, say, a teacher of trumpet. The good teacher will take into account the journey of the beginner and the sorts of issues and queries that naturally arise in his or her experience. This is to work from below. Ultimately, however, the teacher has to make a normative judgment about the practice of trumpet playing into which the beginner is initiated. This is a judgment that stands above the competence and capacity of the beginner to supply. It is a judgment provided by the insider who has come to recognize the prescriptive requirements of a good player.

Likewise, in Christian initiation, good judgments have to be made on two fronts at once. On the one side we need to take into account the queries and concerns of those who are becoming disciples of Jesus Christ. Here we have to listen and attend to the concerns of the potential disciple. Equally, a good judgment has to be made about the normative requirements for the practice of discipleship. In this instance we focus on the internal logic of initiation into the kingdom. This cannot be determined by the disciple but by those entrusted with his or her formation in the faith. Ideally the outcome will be a decision about the content of initiation, a decision that will take both sorts of factors into account and will, therefore, be both faithful and effective. The outcome will seek to enumerate the characteristic issues that need to be worked through, the questions that naturally arise, and the materials and practices that need to be handed over to the new disciple.

Let me cut to the chase at this stage and provide the conclusions to my own deliberations. From my own observations, reflections, and experience over the last ten years or so I think that we can group the issues that naturally arise as people attempt to go to school in Christian discipleship and that dovetail with the logic of initiation into eight distinct categories.[10] In each case I shall propose a cryptic account of the kind of questions that arise and the kind of answers I think should be given.

1. What is the good news which is the necessary foundation of all the calls to discipleship? The good news is that God's kingdom has arrived in the life, death, and resurrection of Jesus Christ who has poured out God's Holy Spirit on those who repent and believe. In this instance the concern is to get some sort of hold on the gospel which serves as the foundation for the life of the church.

2. What kind of experience should I expect to undergo if I repent and believe the gospel? Precisely the kind of experience that is tailor-made for the person's own unique journey toward the living God. In this case we are taking up the issue of the rich dynamic of personal conversion as a person turns in radical repentance and faith to accept Jesus Christ as Savior and Lord.

3. What kind of worldview will I adopt if I become a follower of Jesus Christ? Surely the worldview summed up in the classical creeds of the church, in which the core is belief in the Triune God of the Christian tradition. Here we are reaching for a meaty summary of what the people of God over time have come to see as the intellectual effects of acknowledging the cognitive force of God's great acts of salvation in the incarnation and in Pentecost.

4. What kind of life am I expected to live if I become a Christian? A life of loving God with all one's mind, soul, and will, and loving one's neighbor as oneself. It is within the horizon of this kind of life that one commits oneself to the embrace of bearing the cross out of joyful obedience to Christ. In this instance we are providing a substantial and accurate summary of the ethics of the gospel.

5. How do I relate to others who are making the same journey to God through Jesus Christ on which I am embarking? By being baptized into the

---

10. Most of these issues have arisen as I have worked in actual catechesis, seeking to help local churches ground people in the faith — often for the first time through a program called Basic Christianity, which I developed in collaboration with The First United Methodist Church of Uvalde, Texas.

church and joining in a community of praise, adoration, and service. Here we are recognizing both the human need to be a member of a community and the inescapability of the emergence of a new community in response to the arrival of the kingdom in Jesus.

6. How am I to be empowered to play my part in the kingdom of God? By receiving the sanctifying gift of the Holy Spirit and embracing those gifts and graces that the Holy Spirit distributes sovereignly and freely on Christ's subjects. In this case we are drawing attention to the work of the Holy Spirit in sanctifying and equipping disciples to embody the new life made visible in the incarnation.

7. How am I ever going to be sustained as a disciple of Jesus Christ, given my own wayward dispositions and given the varied assaults of evil I am bound to encounter? By deploying in good faith the many means of grace that are available to nurture one in faith and obedience to God. In this instance we are coming to terms with the natural fear of falling away from faith and drawing attention to the myriad resources available to sustain discipleship in the world as we know it.

8. How do I know that in embracing this way of life I have committed myself to the truth about myself, the world, and God? Answering this may take a lifetime of thought and will only be fully known in the life of the kingdom to come. Christians begin by realizing that we walk by faith and not by sight, and that the deep foundation for the truth we have embraced is the revelation of God articulated by a restored reason and shaped by the varied experiences of the people of God. In this case we are beginning to wrestle with the epistemological and apologetic issues that readily arise for persons raised in a culture with a highly developed sense of competing intellectual options.

Perceptive readers will have noted by now that we can name these issues in a variety of ways. The first deals with the gospel; the next five in turn deal with experiential, intellectual, moral, social, and operational dimensions of Christian initiation. The last two focus on the psychological and cognitive questions that naturally arise in the mind of the new disciple in the West. If we neglect any of these, or if we focus on one set at the expense of the others, we can pretty much predict the outcome in the lives of Christian disciples. If we focus merely on the gospel at the expense of the rest, we will have Christians who never get beyond the first steps of Christian existence.[11] If we focus on the moral and ignore the intellectual, we

---

11. This is the theme of the early chapters of Hebrews.

shall have activists who can make little or no sense of the content of Christian doctrine. If we focus on the intellectual and ignore the moral we shall have legions of dead orthodox on our hands. If we attend only to the importance of church membership and the spiritual disciplines, we shall have nominal Christianity in abundance. If we concentrate only on the richness of Christian experience but ignore the intellectual challenges represented by queries about the rationality of the faith, we shall end with superficial and irrelevant enthusiasts unable to give a reason for the hope that is within them. If we focus only on queries about reflective rationality we shall have networks of eggheads cut off from the treasures of the tradition and deprived of the epistemic practices of the church. What I am seeking to depict overall, then, is the richness and many-sidedness of Christian initiation as displayed when we imaginatively place ourselves in the shoes of those who are undergoing the challenge of Christian initiation and when we explore the intrinsic grammar of initiation. It is my contention that any serious ministry of initiation should cover the territory I have designated.

Two Concluding Comments

I have time for two concluding comments. The first has to do with dealing with the unfaithfulness and even corruption of the church. The second relates to pedagogy.

Corruption and unfaithfulness in the church are healed not by abandoning the church and going in search of the kingdom outside the church but precisely by returning to fresh initiation into the mysterious reality of the kingdom within the church. What could be more relevant here than relearning the treasures of the kingdom by the making of new disciples? On the one hand, such activity is one step in the recovery of the apostolic identity of the church. To begin again to make new disciples is to begin in that very act to recover the apostolic face of the church, for apostolic identity is captured as much by following the apostles in what they did as by holding to what they believed. On the other hand, such activity is a crucial factor in apostolic renewal. Just as teachers suffering from intellectual amnesia can return to the basics of their discipline in the very teaching of a new group of students, so can the church return to its own most holy calling in the very act of making disciples of Jesus Christ. Indeed one way to breathe new life into a dying church is to expose it to the freshness of new converts who through the ministry of the church are finding new life in Christ. John Wesley discovered this from experience when the Moravian, Peter Bohler, told him to preach faith until he himself had faith. In the very preaching and sharing of the gospel we can relearn its mysteries and treasures.

The deep assumption governing this conviction is that God has promised to meet with those who seek him, and most especially he has promised to meet those who seek him where he has covenanted to be found. Few have stated this more graphically than Luther.

> . . . if God were to bid you pick up a straw or to pluck out a feather with the command, order, and promise that thereby you would have forgiveness of all sin, grace, and eternal life, should you not accept this joyfully and gratefully, and cherish, prize, and esteem that straw and that feather as a higher and holier possession than heaven and earth? No matter how insignificant the straw and the feather may be, you would nonetheless acquire through them something more valuable than heaven and earth, indeed, than all the angels, are able to bestow on you. Why then are we such disgraceful people that we do not regard the water of baptism, the bread and the wine, that is, Christ's body and blood, the spoken word, and the laying on of man's hands for the forgiveness of sins as such holy possessions, as would the straw and the feather, though in the former, as we hear and know, God himself wishes to be effective and wants them to be his water, word, hand, bread, and wine, by means of which he wishes to sanctify and save you in Christ, who acquired this for us and who gave us the Holy Spirit from the Father for this work?[12]

We have now cleared the way for a final comment on the pedagogy of making disciples. There is no recipe to be followed here other than this general rule: The church needs to develop sensitive ways of initiating new disciples into the riches of the kingdom. At one end of the spectrum we need the skill of spiritual directors working patiently with individuals, one at a time; some people's needs are so unique that they can be met only by attending to the particulars of their situation. At the other end, the church has had long experience with various kinds of people who together as groups can be systematically taught the treasures and mysteries of the kingdom. The grammar of initiation has been sufficiently identified, and the needs of initiates sufficiently known, to allow the devising of truly effective programs and ministries. What is needed throughout is creativity

---

12. *Luther's Works*, vol. 41, p. 172.

and cheerfulness. Happily both of these, together with everything else we need, are furnished and nourished by the providence of God in creation and history, by the compassion of the Son in his death and resurrection, and by the energies of the all-holy and good and life-giving Spirit.

Contributors

WILLIAM J. ABRAHAM, Professor of Theology, Perkins School of Theology, Southern Methodist University, Dallas, Texas

CARL E. BRAATEN, Executive Director, Center for Catholic and Evangelical Theology, Northfield, Minnesota

JOHN H. ERICKSON, Professor of Canon Law and Church History, St. Vladimir's Orthodox Seminary, Crestwood, New York

GERHARD O. FORDE, Professor of Systematic Theology, Luther Seminary, St. Paul, Minnesota

ROBERT W. JENSON, Senior Scholar for Research, Center of Theological Inquiry, Princeton, New Jersey

RICHARD LISCHER, Professor of Homiletics, The Divinity School, Duke University, Durham, North Carolina

RICHARD A. NORRIS JR., Professor Emeritus of Church History, Union Theological Seminary, New York, New York

K. PAUL WESCHE, Priest, St. Herman's Orthodox Parish, Minneapolis, Minnesota

SUSAN K. WOOD, Associate Professor of Theology, St. John's University, Collegeville, Minnesota

DAVID S. YEAGO, Associate Professor of Systematic Theology, Lutheran Theological Southern Seminary, Columbia, South Carolina